NO TAMING
OF THE
ENTHUSIAST

NO TAMING
OF THE
ENTHUSIAST

A SCENIC ROUTE
INTO COMPUTER SCIENCE

MARIA (MARIJKE) KEET

PORCUPINE PRESS

Johannesburg

Published in 2021 by
Porcupine Press
PO Box 2756
Pinegowrie, 2123
South Africa
admin@porcupinepress.co.za
www.porcupinepress.co.za

POD ISBN 978-1-9284-5589-9

Cover design and page layout: wim@wimrheeder.co.za
Set in 11 point on 15 point, Cambria
Printed and bound by Imaging Solutions, Cape Town

CONTENTS

INTRODUCTION

Good girls go to heaven, bold ones go everywhere.

This was the title of a book I read in my early 20s, and already it was an apt fit – the part about boldly going everywhere, that is. It got me into university to study an interesting topic rather than what the school's career adviser deemed a good choice for nice girls. That, in turn, opened up a few more doors, although at times those doors only gave way after some pushing or creating something that could pass for a key.

The trip to China was a coincidence. I wrote an article that was accepted for the International Conference on Granular Computing that happened to have been organised in the provincial city of Nanchang in the south-east of China that year, just like it happened to be in, among others, San Francisco in 2007. Not that I spoke any Chinese, but the organisers had assured me that a few people at the airport and in the conference hotel would speak a little English that probably would be sufficient to arrive at the conference. All I had to do was print out a page with some Chinese characters on it – I had no idea what they said, as this was before a functioning Google Translate – show it to a taxi driver and everything would work out. It did.

That trip went considerably more smoothly than travelling the north side of the shore of Lake Titicaca in Peru. My copy of Lonely Planet's *Peru* said there should be a bus leaving in the *madrugada* twice a week that would get you to the border with Bolivia on market days, and from there you should be able to catch a ride with a truck to La Paz, but the travel guide's author had heard it from hearsay only. There was a bus. I missed it. My understanding of *madrugada*, 'early in the morning', was 6 - 7 am, whereas theirs was 4 am. Some residents in the village, which was called Moho, said I could walk the distance to the border and still catch the truck. Experienced in walking with a backpack, off I went. The views were stunning and the people in the hamlets I passed were friendly and curious. By the end of the day, on the dark side of dusk, I hadn't reached any border. When I knocked on the door of the first house of the next hamlet, Tilaly, to ask for water, they invited me a stay to wait for the next bus. I gladly accepted the offer. It was a better plan than setting up a tent in the near dark. It was 1996. The village had just got electricity, which meant a few streetlights in the main street, and they were excited: with the curtains open they could now read and do things at night, rather than rely on candles.

Three days later, on the next market day, I made it to the border with the next bus, and travelled on to La Paz in the back of a truck packed with Bolivians and goats and sheep. Later I returned to Lima to conduct lab experiments on the digestibility of sweet potato.

To help warn other people to not do the stupid things I did, I took up Lonely Planet's invitation to mail them feedback to improve on their guidebook. The terrible level of English writing notwithstanding, they were pleased with the additional information, and they gave me a voucher to choose the next Lonely Planet book for free. I picked the one for Ireland, where I was offered my first job abroad – one of those jobs where women are paid substantially less than their male counterparts. Nevertheless, it was fun to work with those colleagues, and the knowledge and skills

I gained there enabled me to move on to greener pastures on the Emerald Isle.

Neither of the experiences in China or Peru had me really worried or anxious or afraid. The Dutch language, my mother tongue (first/home language), does not have a word for or even the concept of the US-English 'clusterfuck'. It's the opposite, rather: *je loopt niet in zeven sloten tegelijk* (you won't walk into seven ditches at the same time). In other words, something may go wrong, but not everything and not completely, so the situation is salvageable.

The attitude that comes with that assumption helps. It was useful as a mantra during the inter-rail trip from the Netherlands to Bulgaria where I went to attend a seminar on culture in Europe, especially the part where we travelled through a Romania that was still very much haunted by the ghost of its last dictator, Nicolae Ceauşescu. My travel companion and I escaped as soon as possible. For good measure, 'the land of the free' wasn't much better when I tried once again to mix business with pleasure by visiting a former colleague and friend after attending and presenting my research at a bioinformatics conference in San Diego in 2005. The prevailing atmosphere was still the post-2001 'terrorists this, that, and the other', so a degree specialising in microbiology, a thesis on terrorism (peace negotiations, more precisely) for a different degree, and being enrolled in a PhD programme in computer science should have sounded a few alarm bells. I had a nagging feeling and continuous unease that The System would grab me. Other people were worried for me, too, which added to my worry. But I wasn't frisked or thrown in jail and I did manage to visit my friend in San Francisco, although the idyllic-looking Greyhound bus of Hollywood movies turned out to be overrated.

This book is not about the awesomeness, and some trials and tribulations, of travelling, although they do come into it along the way. From obstructions in the Dutch village where I grew up to Cape Town where I live now, I ended up in computer science. More specifically, I am currently employed as a professor in computer science at the – by all university rankings – best university of Africa. To be precise, the title is 'Professor', the rank is 'associate'. I am not in the top 1% of computer science professors world-wide, but I have received a few awards here and there and I fare well internationally. I own a house, which I paid for with my own hard-earned money. In the little spare time I have, I dance, read books, exercise, and try to keep up my small garden. Unlike many professors and writers, I don't have 'a supportive wife, two kids, and a dog', just in case you were wondering when they'd turn up in the picture – they won't, as I'm not a lesbian and I don't like dogs. I suppose there may be a possible world where I end up as an old cat lady, but it's not the road I plan to take.

Does all this define me? No, but I'm sure you have formed a picture and an opinion already.

And you, who are you? Perhaps you are a family member, a friend or acquaintance, a nosy stranger or bored passer-by, a current or former colleague or student, or a teenager wondering how one can end up as a professor in a STEM (Science, Technology, Engineering, Mathematics) field. Or perhaps not. Perhaps you are an opponent who is so wound up that you are willing to spend precious time reading this book trying to search for ideas to conjure up more ammunition by intentional misreading of and twisting what I've written to try to fling some more nonsense and discriminatory stuff at me.

This book is aimed at the former group; the latter are not worth my time. A good girl would not have said that so bluntly, or, better, not at all. But if I'd been a good girl, I likely wouldn't have made it into university in the first place, or at best would have attempted a 'useless degree' and become a housewife with a part-time dead-end job. Statistically, in the Netherlands where I grew up, that is where most women end up, which did not sound appealing to me.

Was being bold worth it?

Oh, yes!

Did I annoy a few people along the way? Of course I did. You can't be friends with everyone who crosses your path, and I would not want to be either. This book is neither for them nor about them. There's an element of self-indulgence to writing a collection of memoir essays, but that is not the main point of why I have spent time writing this book. The main point is this: there are so many prejudices and assumptions about female computer scientists that are simply not true and maybe this book will go some way to contributing to humanising us. There also seems to be a remarkable amount of casual sexism going around that's not conducive to constructing a healthy society and a few illustrations of that may assist in recognising them and therewith subsequently prevent them in the long run. It also gives you a peek into the kitchen to discover how one can end up as a science prof despite obstructions and thanks to opportunities. Mine is just one journey and this is my attempt to share with you the very winding road I have travelled. In pseudocode style,

If you want to discover that road, with its bends, detours, potholes and whatnot, *then* stop reading this introduction now and proceed to the next chapter, about soldering at school.

Else if you want to stay on this page, *then* I will give you first a sneak peek by cherry-picking from my resumé.

Else close this book and pass it on to another reader.

....

I grew up in a small Catholic village in the south-east of the Netherlands, studied in the leftist world-improver town of Wageningen in the centre of the country, lived, worked and/or studied in Peru, Ireland, the UK, Italy, and South Africa, and spent at least a few weeks in several other countries, including Germany, Cuba, and Argentina. In my post-secondary education I went from food science to IT courses to computer science, sprinkled with interior design and peace and development studies. I also learned a handful of languages. I progressed from a few uninspiring consulting and tech support jobs to the somewhat more interesting position of test engineer and then associate professor. And, no, my parents did not pay for all my degrees (none, actually), and the cost of most of my travels came either out of my own pocket or because my employer at the time paid most or all of it.

With respect to IT and computing, it turns out that you can succeed in computer science without being a *Star Wars*-loving, pizza-eating, Coke-drinking 'brogrammer' at age 10, or 20, or ever. Partially related to that, since computing is, perhaps, more internationally oriented than some other professions and scientific disciplines: travelling the world is fascinating and underrated by those who prefer to stay put. And somewhat relevant to both previous topics: sure,

I did kick against some sacred cows and I have no regrets about that. Come to think of it, I should kick some more.

Was I drenched in privilege? No. Of course one can compare it to worse. I was not, for instance, a girl in a broken home in a poor township such as Hanover Park – which is located a few kilometres from where I live now – with drugs and gangs and poverty and almost daily shootings. I grew up in the Netherlands, in the social-democratic 'socialist decade' that had abolished class and race. There was a comparatively good education system at the foundation and education was mostly free for everyone. I consistently had more than one meal per day. And in my formative years I did not have to put up with the double whammy of the after-effects of apartheid.

Nowadays, my situation growing up would be categorised as the lower echelons of middle class. Just because there are people who can piss further in the misery contest does not imply that I must have been privileged. Compared to many of my contemporaries and colleagues, I answer that accusation with a resounding No. I was not privileged, not at all. To get where I am today was an uphill battle for me, with many obstacles of disadvantage, of which only a few of a certain type pass the review here.

This book is not an autobiography and so the order of the chapters and their content isn't exactly chronological. To better orientate the reader, I begin each chapter by setting 'the stage', roughly indicating time, place, and context. The chapters are grouped into three parts. Part One touches on some of those unfair states of affairs one starts to encounter in one's youth, the ones that are begging to be kicked against. Part Two is about learning a lot more, yet still expecting that things will go better for my generation, despite encountering some cracks. Part Three boils down to the tiring reality that little has changed for women in STEM. And, without a revolution of some sort, change won't ever go any faster. In the meantime, one either puts up with all the nonsense or leaves. Rather than talking the talk from the sidelines, I am walking the walk and this book is my two cents towards the revolution. By writing it, I am talking the walk and walking the talk too.

That said, despite the few headlines on trailblazing women and from the view of the inner workings, it's still insufficient for getting that revolution going. Progress made may at best be categorised as a slow-moving evolution.

After all the travels and working and living in different countries, the motto of the shield of the Netherlands – *Je maintiendrai* (I will maintain) – seems as apt as ever.

....

There's the usual disclaimer for memoir essays. The events recorded in this book are those I remember to the best of my ability and some people mentioned by name or described indirectly may have a different take on those events. I meant no harm in anything I said, and, in case of negative remarks (that are already sanitised and kinder due to the wear and tear of time), thus certainly not more than the harm they did unto themselves already. Some names of people have been changed and certain details intentionally left vague to protect their identity, at least to some degree. Any translations of conversations from Dutch, German, Spanish, and Italian into English are my own translations and are, by the very nature of translations, approximations of the original.

PART ONE

BRING ON THOSE HURDLES - I JUMP

1

SEGREGATED SOLDERING

The Stage: 1980s – The Netherlands; Ireland too

The 'makeable society' – as if it's merely Lego playtime to build a house – was constructed in the Netherlands. I was expected to become a solid brick in one of its pillars once I'd grown up. I didn't think so.

There was no escaping starting off in one of its pillars, however. For instance, there's a Catholic pillar, where you are born into a Catholic nuclear family, attend a Catholic school, watch and listen to Catholic public broadcasting, and celebrate carnival. There is a similar pillar for each of the various flavours of Protestantism, and any religion as long as there are enough people to join in. Humanism is also an option.

I was born to a Catholic 'heating technician and his wife', according to my unabridged birth certificate – not to a woman who happened to have a husband – in a Catholic village, which, in the 1970s-1980s, had around 6 500 inhabitants. At that time it was known that the village itself had been in existence for at least 1 000 years – in later years, when a new quarter was being added to the village, evidence (urns) of previous societies was found during the excavation of a field, dating back 3 000 years.[1] The village

---

[1] https://www.omroepbrabant.nl/nieuws/2474689/eeuwenoud-urnenveld-gevonden-bij-toekomstige-nieuwbouwwijk (last accessed 6 May 2021).

had a castle with a baron and baroness, which gave it a character and vibe of its own, mixed in with commuter-town characteristics, as quite a number of men commuted to work in the next town or the city. DAF Trucks and Philips were the major employers.

I was enrolled at the nearby Catholic kindergarten and primary school when I turned four. It wasn't the worst of the three Catholic schools in the village. There was one that used to be run by the nuns that still had that smell of the anti-intellectual past hanging around in the building. My school was a new school in a new quarter of the village with a largely young team of teachers of Baby Boomer age who assumed they were progressive. Moreover, it was a five-minute walk from where I lived: cross a street, walk diagonally over a field, cross another two streets and there it was with all its pretensions and aspirations, surrounded by a playground, and with fallow land behind it that stretched out to the 'forest'. The village was surrounded by a collection of trees – a forest by our standards – on my side of the village, a large heather field on the far side of the built-up area, and farming fields diagonally yonder to the south.

The notion of countryside is somewhat relative, with the next towns within cycling distance, trains passing through – the *sneltrein* (fast train) swooshed by but the *stoptrein* (stop train) stopped – and the highway ramp was only three kilometres away. On a nice Sunday afternoon, we sometimes cycled down to Belgium and back. The monastery at the border sold beer and chocolate and there was an ice-cream cart. Shops in the Netherlands were closed on Sundays in those years.

School was from Monday to Friday, with Wednesday

afternoon off. The morning session ran from 08:30 to either 12:00 or 12:30 and the afternoon classes were from 13:30 to 15:30. One of the subjects taught during one of the afternoons was arts and crafts, which could be learning how to draw, paint, sew, or knit, make some quasi-recognisable shapes with clay and so on. You could make a clay ashtray and no one would bat an eyelid. In the lower grades, the school management decided for you what the arts and crafts tasks were; in the higher grades, we got to choose. Well, more precisely, a few times per year we were allowed to fill in a form with our preferences and we would then be allocated to the arts lessons. Those forms almost always had drawing and painting, thread art (the same circle of nails with sewing thread, over and over again), macramé (making artsy knots with sisal threads, in the shape of an octopus), woodwork, and knitting.

When I was in 5th grade, a new topic was introduced: soldering. The teachers weren't sure how it would work out regarding safety the first time they ran it, and so 'therefore it is open to a small group of boys only', as it was stated in the announcement. It went all right and the small group of boys who got to try out soldering were excited about it, so it was set to continue to be offered.

Mildly miffed that it was only available to boys, I sort of patiently waited until the next round of filling in the preferences form. I put soldering as my first choice. The outcome: 'Due to popular demand, the soldering class is oversubscribed.' The list that was distributed with that announcement read (abridged) something like this: 'Tim, Bram and Harry are in. Dennis and Marijke are on the waiting list.'

I was disappointed but accepted that it was possible

that the class was oversubscribed – the basement venue was smaller than the classrooms and by then a larger group of boys were interested in it thanks to word of mouth on the coolness of soldering. I decided to try again next time and meanwhile make the most of – yet again! – the thread art class to which I was allocated. The next announcement was similar to the first: 'Due to popular demand ...' only this time the list read: 'Dennis, Marco and Harry are in. Tim, Marijke and Peter are on the waiting list.'

That didn't look fair – not at all. But back to the thread art class I went, hitting more nails into wood, painting the wood, and then stringing the nails with thread in two or three colours. The third time, it was: 'Tim, Peter and Henry are in. Marijke and Nico are on the waiting list.'

Hey! Boys get to jump the queue and get in twice even!

I had lost all my patience by then, so I started prodding the teachers. Surely if it was a proper queue, it would have been my time several times already? Nah, came the response, they were still a bit cautious. After all, 'just because it was without incidents a few times doesn't mean it's generally safe' was their reasoning. And so it went on, back and forth, for a while. Eventually, over one year later, I came straight out and asked my 6th grade teacher, who was one of the Baby Boomers who thought he was going with the times, what was going on here. Eventually he admitted: 'It's just not open to girls. But,' he continued, 'isn't it nice of us that we put you in the thread art group instead each time?' I grimaced to indicate that I was not convinced, and he added, by way of explanation: 'There you can use a hammer to hit nails, and that's manly too, no?'

It didn't even occur to them that my wanting to be in the soldering class had nothing to do with doing 'manly' things, nor with wanting to do things I was not allowed to do for the sake of it. I wanted to learn to do something new. I had rotated through all the other arts and crafts tons of times and either was good enough at them (compared to the rest in the class or to my own satisfaction) or I truly wasn't interested in them anymore. I was bored with those other options. The gender-based policy made me want to do the soldering class more, sure, but it was not even close to being the main reason. It still annoys me that an institute of learning was anti-learning and twisted the concept of the waiting list – and got away with it.

This is irrespective of the flawed arguments used to justify such a stance and the fact that it fitted within a broader attitude of anti-intellectualism at that school, De Merlebos. To illustrate that claim, I'll pick non-randomly another topic among the possible choices: mathematics. Sometime during the school year in Grade 3, I completed all the maths exercises and all the Grade 3 extra exercise cards and there was still some of the year left to get through somehow. Luckily, I received approval from the teacher to try the Grade 4 extra exercise cards for the mathematics exercises. They were an interesting challenge, and I completed at least half of those, too, although not all of them 100% correctly. The next year in Grade 4, when the rest of the class was still trying the regular exercises and the odd extra exercise card, I had re-done that half to make sure I could breeze through them, and I completed the remaining exercise cards. It was about halfway in the school year. I was hoping for the same kind of deal as the year before. With a certain eagerness and pride in my voice, I approached the teacher. 'May I go to the 5th grade class to fetch some extra exercise cards?' I asked.

'No. You're in Grade 4, and you shall do Grade 4 work,'

the teacher responded. I tried to argue.

'But I've done the extra cards, and more than half of them twice already! *And* I completed them mostly or fully correctly,' I pointed out, aware of the slight desperation in my voice.

The response? 'Then do them again.'

As if the real message was 'Sit in class and waste your time, succumb to boredom or something, but either way we shall prevent you from learning too much or too fast'. It was a recipe for asking for trouble, rather. This was supposedly a modern school. It was a new one that had been built from scratch in the early 1970s, so there were no entrenched school traditions to uphold. Yet, new and modern, let alone progressive or visionary, apparently do not go hand in hand together.

....

Fast-forward to the early 2000s in Ireland, where I was enrolled for an MA in Peace and Development studies at the University of Limerick. One of the courses was about gender and peace. With Ireland not particularly famous for women's rights and at a time when the Catholic church was in the news for all the wrong reasons, there was ample discussion material about gender issues. My classmates, much the same as many other people in the world, were under the impression that the Netherlands was progressive on gender equality – after all, abortion was legal there, so we surely must be ahead, or so went the reasoning. I described to them a few cases where it was clearly not so, one of which was the soldering saga.

The instant response was 'Yes! Oh! We had that too! Not

for soldering, but we weren't even allowed to do woodwork!' Woodwork was a school subject that was offered only at boys' schools, not girls' schools; similar grumblings were voiced about technical drawing. They had to knit and cook and such, as part of home economics. One of the few guys in the class pondered that he might have liked to try those too, out of curiosity. I guess it was slightly better in the village where I grew up then. I had to deal with a backward school, whereas Ireland seemed to be backward even at the national level of state policies on education. One whole generation obstructed. A step up from not being allowed to go to school, indeed, but that doesn't mean such systemic gender profiling (discrimination, really) is fine.

That conversation took place in 2003 and there was not a lot of material online to verify whether the notion of boys-only or girls-only subjects was state policy in Ireland or not. A quick search for boys and girls schools in the Limerick area in late 2020 showed that school subject practices hadn't improved very much.[2] The girls' school whose curriculum I was able to access online still didn't offer technical drawing (now called design and communication graphics), technology or the like. The boys' school in nearby Charleville not only offered technical drawing but also construction studies and, lo and behold, home economics.

A national curriculum, however, is precisely that. It doesn't say anything about differentiation between boys' and girls' schools. It's individual schools' management that imposes these areas of difference on the learners who attend their schools. My generation is, or should be, the generation now in charge of those schools – so what's wrong with them?!

---

[2] The ones consulted with online information include https://colaistenanonagle.ie/senior-cycle.html in Limerick and https://charlevillecbs.com/senior-cycle/ in nearby Charleville (last accessed in December 2020).

2

ALTAR BOYS AND GIRLS

The Stage: 1980s – The Netherlands;
same Catholic village

'*We moeten consistent beleid voeren. Ik ben gewoon tegen,*'
I said during one of the Progressive Student Party meetings
(We have to follow through consistently with the policy.
I am against it.). A party member thought my statement
wonderful, typed it up and printed it, and taped the sheet
to a wall of the student union building, lest we forget and
be swallowed by The System. It had to do with a topic about
a possible university management configuration against
which the party had voted over the years and nothing of the
core of the proposal had changed substantially. Whether
the university organisation should become pillars or
rhombi or stay in a mesh-like configuration was good for
long debates, but not the barricades.

There were other themes that were worthy of protest. I
both joined and instigated a fine number of protests in the
Netherlands, and participated in a few abroad. Before that,
at school, it was just me as instigator. My first lobbying and
protest action was when I attended primary school: let's
take on the Church, because why start small.

We're in that Catholic village still. It didn't feel overly
religious at the time. Sure, there were the church bells
ringing every hour, but that was useful for finding out the

time without wearing a watch or asking around. Going to church only at Christmas was borderline acceptable and you could expect mild criticism from your classmates that that was too infrequent. Few went every Sunday, though, and the daily morning mass was attended by 10 to 20 old people and an occasional devout younger adult.

It did feel slightly off that there was the 'Protestant graveyard', as it was colloquially known, which was situated outside of the built-up area and bordered some agriculture fields on a back road to the neighbouring village. 'Non-Catholics' who died were not allowed to be buried in any graveyard within the built-up area of the village, for not having been and died a Catholic. Practically, it meant that all Protestants, Jews, and Catholic suicides ended up in the Protestant graveyard. Its official name was 'general cemetery'. There were no villagers of other religious persuasions as far as I knew, other than one Sikh temp exchange employee. We assumed he'd be shipped back to India for burial if it came to that. It was the way things were. Just like the baron and baroness had owned the area in the feudal system that came before democracy – and which had been abolished in due course – it was not to be questioned.

In that ambience, and supported by that new Catholic school I attended in the new quarter, we had to do our Holy Communion in spring in 2nd grade (the school year you turn eight), regardless of whether you wanted to or not. If you were at a Catholic primary school, the class planning even made time for it during school time to properly prepare you for it. Those lessons involved some Bible reading and conversations on their deeper meaning, colouring in drawings of some Bible scene, and practice for the Big Day.

Because I had a loud and clear voice and could read relatively well already, I was asked to be one of the three child readers for the Holy Communion mass. This required some additional preparation. Regarding my conviction on whether I was religious or not, that was another matter: I had hedged my bets, just in case He might exist, but I wasn't too convinced. The presents and family visits that came with the event were appealing and induced the perception that it must be something important and perhaps not something to mess with. All our family lived far away up north on the other side of the main rivers in the country and they came over once or twice a year, three times at most, to visit us, but now they were coming, all the way just for me, which was a first – well, second, but I can't remember my birth and baptism.

A few days after the Communion, it was announced in class that the boys were allowed to become altar boys in the nearby church, St Martinus, which was the largest of the three churches in the village. Our school fell within its parish. There were several arguments brought to bear to try to persuade the boys to become altar boys. We girls had to sit in and listen to it all but we were excluded from signing up. Of course, there's the argument of serving God and church, but there were perks associated with the duty too. First, altar boys were allowed to come to school by bicycle when they were scheduled for assisting in the daily morning mass for a week at a time; the rest of us mere mortals had to walk. Furthermore they were allowed to arrive late in the morning: class started at 08:30, but they could rock up at 08:45 or even 09:00. When you're eight years old, these are no trivial matters. Second, for bonus points, altar boys were permitted to skip class for weddings and funerals any time in the day, and if that was not enough, sometimes they were invited to the reception or *koffietafel* (a lunch-like meal after a funeral) afterwards if they had done a good job.

I wanted those perks too. It was unfair that boys were allowed to become altar boys, but girls were not. There was no such thing as an altar girl.

I asked both the pastor, the pensive Fr Somers, and the verger, who doubled as a toyshop owner, but the response was the same: girls were simply not fit to be altar girls, just like they couldn't become a pastor, bishop, or pope. That did not sound to me as if it resembled a coherent logical explanation, since they did not even try to explain *why*. Then, a supposedly existing God who presumably thinks that roughly half the world population are lesser entities, can't be a god. Hedging my bets was over and atheism it was, since I refused to accept that I wouldn't be equal but less. Humans were equal, and girls as capable as boys of ringing a bell, or carrying and handing over a chalice, or swinging the frankincense holder, looking solemn and such. Changing this state of affairs was overdue and, in my opinion, the church was wrong. A 'god swap' to Protestantism did not occur to me and anyhow it would not have solved the systemic problem of the Catholic church communicating to girls and women that they were unfit. But how to go about changing things?

I took my bicycle and cycled back to the pastor and the verger in the village centre and tried again. This time I came prepared with more arguments.

Still no. And they started to add to their flawed reasoning.

'Besides,' they pointed out, 'you are the only one asking.

You are the odd one out.'

'No, I'm not. There are other girls in class who agree with me,' I retorted.

'Is that so? We have not seen them. But if it *is* the case, then they, too, will have to go to the verger to ask to be included. If enough girls want to be altar girls, perhaps we might reconsider it.'

This was a typical fob-off, I knew that by now, but in my youthful enthusiasm and determination it was a clarion call to start campaigning. I knew that, like me, some of my other classmates disapproved of the discrimination. My first step was to convince them to go and ask the pastor and the verger. We went a few times, in small groups of two to four learners.

Then there was some canvassing to be done to convince other girls in class that the practice was unfair and likewise to please visit the verger and ask to become altar girls. We encouraged them while they were at it to complain about the fact that girls couldn't be altar girls. It went back and forth for a short while, but soon it was summer holiday time and things quieted down.

Early into the start of 3rd grade in the first few weeks of class in August, the pastor came by with renewed energy to try to recruit boys to become altar boys, as there had not been an overwhelming sign-up. The *ontkerkelijking*, that is, the decrease in practising religion in an organised manner in church, if not secularisation as well, was gradually taking hold. We tried again, adding the shortage of altar boys as an extra argument and pointing out that we could solve this problem if they would only allow girls to apply. Our efforts were to no avail.

We visited the verger multiple times, alone and in small

groups. By Grade 4, we had recruited a few girls from the grade below us. Still no improvement in our chances. As I visited the toyshop a few times a year to buy presents for classmates' birthday parties and some school supplies, whenever I was there, I asked the verger whether there was any progress on the matter. I was already in 5th grade when, asking yet again in the usual way if he had an update for me, the verger told me to go to the pastor, as he had news. The verger did not want to tell me what it was. Veering between excitement and preparation for disappointment, I cycled over to the church, which was about 200 metres from the shop, in search of Fr Somers. The church door was open and he was in.

'Yes, I have news,' he said. 'I had to ask the bishop, who's all the way in Den Bosch …' Den Bosch was the provincial capital some 51.3 kilometres north of our village. When distance is measured in how much time it takes to walk or cycle, 50 kilometres is quite far. 'That took a while, since these are not trivial matters,' Fr Somers said. I waited expectantly. 'The bishop has approved it.'

Finally we were allowed to become altar girls! But there was one last hurdle: unlike the boys, who were naturally gifted to take up the duty, we girls had to go through a six- or seven-week training programme before we could become altar girls. Presumably, we were too clueless and needed some Bible lessons, some talking to and reflecting, and a few dry-runs. We suspected this was the pastor's last attempt to discourage us. The news travelled fast, as any news does in a village. Although some of the girls had lost interest after all the delays, a sizeable number were still interested, if only because it was a victory of sorts.

The task of educating us in the altar girl induction

programme fell on the shoulders of the live-in nun who supported the pastor and the parish, with an occasional drop-in by the pastor himself. Training took place in the richly decorated rectory, with practice in the adjacent church now and then. Grumbling about the different treatment, but determined, we went ahead with the training; about seven or eight of us remained at the end of it. I don't know if any of us was actually religious by then, but we made it and did it.

....

I stayed on until when I was about 14, after which it was too hard to slot me in due to conflicting school rosters and other activities, which happened with most altar boys as well. Still, my first encounter with politics was a victory.

I checked the church information in late 2020 when writing this chapter, as a bit of a gamble to see if I could quickly find out whether it had petered out or whether that step towards equality lived on after me and continued with the new pastor. I was not sure what to expect. What I found online was: '*Welkom zijn jongens en meisjes in de basisschoolleeftijd*' (boys and girls of primary school age are welcome).[3]

That was a pleasant surprise. It's likely that I wasn't the only one who pushed, but I was definitely one of the earlier ones and can claim that I was successful. With some persistent effort and teaming up, change is possible. Hooray.

---

[3]https://parochienicasius.nl/index.php/werkgroep-heeze (last accessed on 28 December 2020).

3

TAKE MY ADVICE

The Stage: mid-1980s–early 1990s –
The Netherlands; same village; the next towns

Take my advice; I don't use it anyway.
In this case, more precisely, the ones who were *giving* it weren't using it anyway. I am talking about school advice of the variety of where to go next when you're about to finish one. If there was a betting office on such advice giving, who do you think would win – The System or the individuals within it? Let's see.

Any school system in the world has a trajectory of at least primary school and secondary school, and then some form of tertiary education to learn for a job, if you did not already do that in secondary school. So, there is at least one choice point: where to go after primary school. First, which type of school to go to? And second, which school among that type?

I knew what I wanted, but the choice depended on many factors, some with a heavier weighting than others. School ranking in a league table was not one of them, as there were no league tables. All schools were public schools, so there was not that sort of problem or consideration to be given either. There were other strategies to try to figure it out. There's the grapevine when you have older siblings; there's the option to visit the schools during their respective open days to smell the ambience; there's the choice between religious/multi-denominational/non-religious; and there's the logistics of how to travel there daily (by bicycle, mainly). The very first determiner, however, is the level – lower, middle, higher or preparatory scientific – and how to figure out the right level. I might have ended up earning a PhD and becoming a professor, but that does not say anything of 'back in the day'.

Even in the 1980s, The System knew all too well that primary school teachers and some parents, too, can be a bit backward in their thinking and influence the child's choice to their detriment. For instance, when parents have a working-class status in a stratified society, when it comes to their children, they may not promote achieving higher aims and therefore they may send their child to a lower-level secondary school on the understanding of accepting one's lot. Or a teacher may give the parents the advice that the *lagere huishoudschool* (lower home economics school) is a fine choice for their daughter, where she can learn to become a good housewife. Such a *lagere huishoudschool* was the only secondary school in our village when I was in my last year of primary school.

My older brother was at a school that was relatively far away, but one he enjoyed going to. The coolest thing about it from my viewpoint was that they offered Russian instead of dead languages – Latin and Greek – and that sounded to me like a clear-headed choice for relevance. I concluded that the school must be sensible. It was at one of the heights of the Cold War, a short while after we had given the Americans the finger when they tried to put nukes in the Netherlands as some pathetic posturing attempt, and there were pop songs about the Russians. Who wouldn't want to learn Russian to see for yourself what they had to say? In addition, my brother had a teacher with a hardcover Frank Zappa appointment calendar, which sounded hip. But it had already been made clear to me that that school was not on the cards: the logistics of travelling to that school was too expensive because of the additional train ticket. While the expense was warranted for my brother because he was an in-between-levels, that was not the case for me, I was told, and therewith not worth the money. Russian language excitement be damned.

The second-closest secondary school was a 'middle general' secondary school (MAVO) in the next town, which was a 5 km bicycle ride away. Some 7.5 km away there was a 'higher general' (HAVO) and 'preparatory scientific' (VWO) secondary school that combined both levels and was multi-denominational. There were more choices in the nearest big city, Eindhoven, from Catholic to Protestant to posh to technikon, but they were at least 12 km on the bicycle – there and back, every day of the week, 40 weeks a year, regardless of the weather.

But there was still the question of how to determine the 'appropriate' level of secondary school for me, and where within those levels I'd end up. Let's start with 0:0 for The System versus the individual adults in it.

Once upon a time, too many bright girls were sent to those housewife-to-be secondary schools and teachers' advice and parents were blamed for that sorry state of affairs. The solution The System proposed, possibly in no small part thanks to feminists who went before me, was a test – called the CITO Toets – which was done in the last year of primary school, nationwide. Then, in qualifying for a secondary school, the highest advice would count. If your teacher was a sexist pig and gave the advice of, say, 'middle general' school but your test results indicated you were actually intelligent enough for higher general secondary education (a score of ≥540 out of 550) or preparatory scientific education (a score of ≥545), your teacher's advice was allowed to be ignored and you could land in that higher level secondary school. It worked the other way around in a similar way: if your test results were lower than the teacher estimated you would obtain, you probably had a bad hair day when you took the test and so let's ignore the test and trust that teacher. If you were a *girl* with a bad hair day, you were screwed, unless you were a *good girl*, in which case you might be lucky to elicit the benefit of the doubt.

I was not a good girl, but at least I had a fine day with that CITO Toets and the questions were easy enough to finish before the time was up. My teacher? *He* had a bad hair day, at best. My teacher was that same one of the no-soldering and on top of that he preferred to give conservative advice, because 'in that way there will be less disappointment later on'. The Dutch language has a phrase for 'benefit of the doubt', but, with a probability bordering on certainty, it wasn't in his vocabulary. The advice I received was 'higher general secondary education', with a slight chance of possibly 'preparatory scientific education', as that would be enough to allow me entry into a higher/prep combination school if I really wanted that, but not a prep-only one. My CITO Toets score? 550, the maximum score possible. And I was the only one in the 50-odd cohort who obtained a score of 550 and apparently even so across all four schools in the village that year. But no, the teacher said to my parents, he would not revise his advice. Somehow, he said, I must have been extremely lucky. I wasn't. Because it wasn't certain I was going to be able to take the CITO Toets because it might coincide with my grandfather's celebration of 40 years of being a grocer and 40 years being married to my grandmother, and it was his birthday as well, I had done another qualifying test. Same story of top marks. I doubly qualified for any prep school.

1:0 for The System.

....

I went to two open days of schools that were the higher/ prep combination. One was a multi-denominational school that seemed hip, and, most importantly, one where you could choose any combination of exam subjects. The other one was a Catholic school. Already at the entrance it felt oppressive and repulsive to me, before I even was presented with the straitjackets of the programmes they offered. There was the posh school too, but that wasn't even tried, as it was anticipated I would not fit in anyway. So, the nearest combination school it was, after all, with me still swallowing the bummer of not being able to learn Russian.

Six years of preparatory scientific education and I was in my last year. My grades might not have been fabulous, but I had coped – managing a fine balancing act with the many non-school activities, among other distractions. Now it was time to orient and make up my mind about what I wanted to study at university.

I had wanted to become an architect before I could even pronounce the word, but having been exposed to biology and chemistry since 2nd grade, my aims had shifted. So what next? I had visited the nearest university, the Technical University in Eindhoven, to explore the possibilities of studying chemistry. It was a bit of a testosterone bastion (we'll return to that in a later chapter) and anyhow I wasn't interested in inorganic chemistry. I'd also been to an open day at Utrecht University to see if chemistry there was any better and I was also considering biology. The chemistry on offer did not impress me there either and as for biology, I decided that I didn't want to either bore myself memorising taxon names of plants or dissect animals. The school organised trips to other universities to make sure everyone in the class had visited at least one. I found myself having to choose between signing up for a trip to Maastricht University, which was running an experiment on problem-oriented education through teamwork for predominantly non-technical degree programmes, or the Technical University of Enschede, so the latter it was. The main thing I remember from that excursion was that there were almost no women on campus and those who were, were 'substitute men' wholly assimilated in some sort of boys-only culture. There was one female student on the tour, and I did not want to end up akin to her.

I had the luminous – or stupid – idea of seeking advice. The secondary school I went to, Strabrecht College, had a 'career advice centre'. Actually it was just a room with a wall full of brochures about university degree programmes of a theoretical or applied nature, staffed by a teacher who thought he was generously doing an additional service alongside his teaching Dutch language and literature. Let's call him Mr Van Dijk. I wasn't too happy it was him. I vividly remembered his unfairness in class in 4th grade when we all had to do a ten-minute talk about some current affairs or science topic and everyone had observed a suspect pattern: Mr Van Dijk seemed to tend to prefer giving higher marks to the boys. During one lecture, there were two talks. First up was friendly and dull Johan, who presented the latest science on cholesterol (dangerous!). He went on and on and on … for nearly 18 minutes. Some students were looking pointedly at their watches, others just dozed off. Second came Lucille, who was a good girl and upbeat. Her talk was well organised, lively and exactly 10 minutes long. The topic she'd chosen was the corpus callosum – the 'road' between the left and the right hemispheres of the brain. According to the research, this 'road' is thicker in women's brains, with more communication happening, thereby suggesting higher intelligence. Everyone was listening to that, for sure – and worrying, once that conclusion was flung in the air and bouncing around in the classroom. What would Mr Van Dijk do? Johan was awarded an 8.5/10 whereas Lucille received a mere 6.5/10! The whole class – boys and girls – gasped audibly at the obvious unfairness of a substantially lower mark for a much better presentation, yet nothing changed.

That was the calibre of the teacher who was tasked with advising learners what to do after secondary school. One wonders what school management's views were. Anyway, I stepped into the careers office to ask for advice and I mentioned my interests. Mr Van Dijk first presented me with a few brochures about degrees in the so-called 'soft sector', such as sociology and history. That was not what I was looking for. I told him so.

'My exam subjects are mainly the "real maths"', I explained: 'and physics, chemistry and biology. Actually I'm looking for a degree where I can combine chemistry and biology.'

'But these degrees are nice, and suitable for you,' Mr Van Dijk said. 'Or look here, maybe law is of interest then?' He fetched another brochure, and then another. He wasn't just not answering my question; he was evading it. To this day, I'm not sure what got into me but then and there I very sternly told him in no uncertain terms that if he didn't give me the career information I was asking for, 'I will go to the rector denouncing you that you are failing in your duty as career adviser!'

Taken aback by my outburst, he muttered a bit, but eventually pulled out a government brochure that listed in one large table all degrees available, with their pre-requisites. He put it on the table and said I could look at that, if I insisted. Then it was a simple matter of scanning which ones had a dot in the chemistry and biology columns. Lo and behold, food science popped into view. A whole new world opened for me.

In hindsight, I should have gone to the rector anyway. I'm fairly sure most of my classmates would not have been as assertive as I was. How many girls did that man send into 'useless' degrees they never wanted to do anyhow? How many potential Nobel Prize winners were terminally obstructed in their pursuits? Universities regularly ask the question: 'why are there not more women in STEM?' One answer to that is: because of bad advice by a prejudiced teacher trying to pass for a career adviser.

....

Having visited Wageningen University on its open day, I was sold – the four-year MSc degree in food science it would be. I was on my way to solving the world food problem. There was that last hurdle of the final exams, or so I thought. I passed with decent marks and definitely a better mark for chemistry than I expected at the start of the year. I had studied hard and the advanced topics in chemistry were exciting, which helped studying as well. One of the two senior chemistry teachers, Mr Bliksem, was at the school when the results came out, to congratulate the graduates and so on. None of us learners knew quite what to make of him, but he had given us the benefit of the doubt with the lesson on the s and p orbitals that was awesome and the extra topic on the histamines was very interesting. He seemed to be pleased I was very interested in it all and that I performed a lot better in the test on those topics compared to the tests about the run-of-the-mill topics. At some level, I thought, we got along fine thanks to that. He congratulated me and was likewise pleasantly surprised at my results.

'What are you going to study?' he asked.

'Food science,' I said with the big smile of someone moving to ever greener pastures.

'Ah, in Den Bosch?'

'Uh, no, in Wageningen.' Not the BSc stream at the Higher Agrarian School that is intended for after the 'higher general' (HAVO) level, but the MSc stream at the Agricultural University in Wageningen that comes after the preparatory scientific (VWO) level that I was right there and then graduating from. I left this to sink in.

'But,' he tried again, 'it is safer to go straight to Den Bosch, rather than having to adjust downward halfway, as then you'll lose out on state financing for your study.'

'But,' I tried, 'the diploma I'm receiving now entitles me to enrol at the university for that degree and I'm surely going to give it a try none the less.'

'Well, it's your risk,' came the disapproving last word.

Yes.

I was accepted into the degree programme, since I qualified with the diploma and the prerequisite exam subjects; no teacher advice is involved in that process.

2:0 for The System.

Everyone who was accepted in a degree programme received a scholarship from the state that was sufficient to live off, buy study books, and pay tuition fees.

3:0 for The System.

Of course, it was one of those instances that made me doubt myself, and I promised myself that if I totally flunked the first trimester, I'd heed Mr Bliksem's advice. I gave up a trip to Jamaica with my then boyfriend and his family so as to be able to do those first trimester exams right before the Christmas break, worrying I might fail and have to switch tertiary institutions and move town again. In fact I did fine – which makes sense: my grades for the prerequisites were fine/good; if I had failed, then perhaps the systems were not aligned. I should have ignored more of those advice-giving teachers.

And I still would like to visit Jamaica.

4

THE COMPUTER TRIES TO DO WHAT IT IS INSTRUCTED TO DO

The Stage: Late 1980s – The Netherlands

On any particular day in the 1980s, a PC was no fun to work with and, besides, using such a human-unfriendly box is not nearly the same as computer science. But what does a young teenager know, who can speak Dutch and a little German and French, but sits in front of an operating system and application software in English? It is possible to be frustrated with computers and computing and all that at a young age, yet appreciate it in due course. Admittedly, the machines can still irritate me immensely on occasion, but my irritation is mainly directed at the managers who instruct the software developers intentionally to build nasty 'features' into the software, or take them away under the pretence of improvements. Those of the 1980s were, perhaps, not bad by malicious intent of the developers, but more because of limitations on the machines' capabilities and limited advances in computing.

Two encounters with near-evil 'features' of yesteryear's user-unfriendly machines I remember vividly to this day. I still resent them. The nasty features, or, rather, bad design, were made worse by the circumstances: being the youngest girl in the household, I was last in line to be allowed access to the PC. Even my brother playing games took precedence over any of my studious activities – 'because it is important for him to become acquainted and familiar with the PC, and while games aren't the best way to do so, he'll pick up something from it'. Jeez! This was in line with the Zeitgeist of the late 1980s, when 'the collapse' was in full swing. The masculinisation of computing (in the West at least) saw women's participation in computing crash down in the early 90s to a low of between 5-15% from their previous heights – in the early to mid-80s – of 30-50% participation. This was largely due to the branding of PCs as boys' toys, stereotyping nerdiness, and the notion that much money can be made with software and therewith inducing a particular version of professionalisation.[4] I knew nothing about all that. I just categorised it under one of the many unfair opinions, prejudices, and decisions adults made. Why would a PC be primarily a thing for boys and men who speak English?! There was no good reason for that that I could see. I deemed that I should have the same rights to access and to find a PC of interest.

Notwithstanding my limited access, one thing I did know about was the PC. Ours was a Philips PC, probably of the P31 series.[5] One of those that took a large floppy disk and to which you could attach a cassette player and play a cassette that had, say, Pac-Man or chess on it. The notion of software localisation had yet to be invented, so both the operating system's commands and all application software was in English. I did not speak a single word of English.

---

[4]The cause being the cultural shift in the mid 1980s, the key components whereof have been well researched. An easily accessible four-minute radio snippet and transcript is available at: https://www.npr.org/sections/money/ 2014/10/21/357629765/when-women-stopped-coding (last accessed on 26 May 2021).
[5]https://www.homecomputermuseum.nl/collectie/philips/ (last accessed on 26 May 2021).

I sort of made do by memorising sequences of letters on the screen and the layout of something, which was a challenge as there were no real graphical user interfaces.

And so it was on *pakjesavond* of the Saint Nicholas celebrations on the 5th of December that I was typing up a poem I had written first on paper. The thing with the Saint Nicholas celebrations is that the present and the poem are supposed to be anonymous and my handwriting would give me away and spoil the surprise. Everyone else had typed up and printed theirs already, and me being last in line, there was little time left to finish it. Alone in the study where the PC had been placed, I painstakingly typed it up in a very early version of WordPerfect – the typing with two fingers variety as I had to search for each letter on the keyboard. And then it was time to print it. That early WordPerfect version, a v3.x it must have been, only had a bunch of shortcut keys and there was no cheat sheet. I couldn't remember which key or key combination it was, so I tried one combination that I could remember. The subsequent human-computer interaction went roughly as follows:

System: shows a dialog box with '[some text I did not understand] [a sequence of letters that does not have p r i n t]?'

Me: Huh? No. Okay, so guessed wrong. Cancel this.

Me: Let's try another combination with a function key.

System: another dialog box pops up with '[some text I did not understand] s a v e [some other text]?'

Me: Nah, darn no, stupid box. Make that message go away. I don't want to store it on disk. I want to transfer it onto a piece of paper and I'm trying to find that key that gives me a box that says something with '... p r i n t ...' So I select 'no'.

System: all text goes away. Cursor blinks on the top left.

Me: a very loud scream ...

Why must the machine be so uncooperative?! A translation to understand what it was saying would have helped. An undo option too. Also, it would have been so much nicer if there had simply been *one* function key to remember which, upon pressing it, would have returned a pop-up with something along the lines of 'Now, dear, what would you like to do with this file? Type [ctrl+F5] to print, [shift+F3] to save, and [alt+F4] to quit' (well, anyway, they are the shortcut codes nowadays).[6] It lists the DOS shortcut keys as F7 for 'close current window' and shift+F7 for 'print', which sounds like a plausible mix-up for the keys I hit that fateful evening some 35 years ago. Quite frankly, there's still no logic to the declared default shortcut keys, and human-computer interaction designers ought to be ashamed of themselves. It isn't even limited to that: currently, in many Windows applications, ctrl+P causes a pop-up window to print the document, but even in the TeXnicCenter application that I'm using to type this book, ctrl+P is 'select paragraph' rather, not to mention the Apple vs Windows shortcut keys.

At the time, I felt it was me failing in my well-meaning attempts to be able to use a PC – this box that seemed to me already then to have a bright future with possibilities beyond my imagination. I know better now, and have done for some 20 years. Of all things computing, harmonisation of shortcut keys is the low-hanging fruit in the smorgasbord of fixing software to make a user's experience so much more pleasurable. And yet it still has not happened. I can assure you that I don't teach my students to come up with

---

[6]https://wptoolbox.com/library/WP_shortcut_keys.pdf (last accessed in December 2020).

unintuitive shortcut key combinations.

After that scream of desperation – why on earth did the function keys have to be cryptic? – teary-eyed, I retyped the whole bloody thing, asked which key it was to print a darn document, and eventually printed it. The computer does what you instruct it to do, not what you want it to instruct it to do. It was a harsh lesson. One thing that's cool about studying computer science is that you will learn that you *can* control the box and *how* to control it, instead of the box controlling you.

But before I got there, there was the other hair-pulling encounter with the uncooperative machine. This problem hasn't been fixed either and it is one of those litmus tests to set the sysadmin and other insiders apart from the average 'luser'. We had to write an essay as a homework assignment, something for Dutch or history or social science class at school, and I wanted to type my essay out on the PC to make it look professional. The first problem was access to the PC, again. I tried early on, but to no avail. The first time I would be able to access it after everyone else was done with it was the evening before the assignment was due when everyone was out. I wasn't fond of deadline surfing, so was not particularly happy, but at least some access was better than no access.

And so that evening I sat down at the PC in the study, intending to launch WordPerfect to start typing up what I had written and finalise the text. The program did not launch. I tried again. And again and again. Double-checking that I hadn't made any typos, double-checking that I'd used the correct commands, double-checking the directory, and so on and so forth.

Still no WordPerfect.

Panic followed, then utter desperation, interspersed with some crying and screaming. I tried other number combinations of the command, like not v4.1 but v5 and v5.1 and the older v3.x. Nothing gave way. There was no 'googling Stackoverflow' as the Web had yet to be invented, no class WhatsApp group to crowdsource the answer, and no 'call a friend' since none of my friends had computers. After freaking out for some two hours and becoming increasingly nervous about that assignment deadline, my father returned home.

'Ah, yes, I may have updated WordPerfect from v4.1 to 4.2 and I didn't tell you.'

Bastard. He knew I had to use WordPerfect for the assignment. Launching wp4.2 worked and I typed and printed late, went to bed late, and handed in my assignment on time the next day. It did look posh compared to the average, even though it was printed out with a mere matrix printer, but if I had had to do that evening again, I would have chosen instead to have written my essay by hand like most of my classmates did. The anguish, frustration, and hatred weren't worth it.

I still dislike those command line prompts with a passion. They all refuse to give away what's hidden behind the cursor and that system stupidly insists on memorisation skills, even when there's a whole computer at one's disposal to memorise trivial stuff.

....

All those frustrations and all that trial and error did give me a step ahead in class nonetheless. In the 3rd or 4th grade of secondary school (around 1989 in my case), we had

IT as a subject, for one hour per week. It was taught by a history teacher who enjoyed playing with a PC whom we had nicknamed Mr Floppy Disk. His fingers were so big we wondered how often he hit two keyboard keys at once. A chemistry lab temporarily doubled as computer classroom, since no regular classroom had enough electricity sockets and IT as a subject at school was still a bit of try and see if it would work out or not. Each square service pillar in the lab had four large tables positioned around it with a PC each and there were two chairs per table. Pair PC use and pair programming was in use long before software engineering elevated it to a concept. There was one matrix printer for the whole class, which was on the teacher's desk in the front of the class.

Grapevine had it that if you'd already used a computer, it would be a boring class. The way I saw it was that it would grant me access to a PC, something I was having difficulty with at home. The question was how to try to maximise this. Perhaps it was sneaky or overly calculating of me, but I tried to team up with a classmate for PC partner whom I knew did not care for computers. This meant that I would be able to play more with the machine, and hopefully learn more. I put the word out. Linda was into ballet and wanted to become a professional dancer, and, importantly, she was trying to strategise how to avoid having to do any IT in the IT class, or at least as little as possible. It was an easy deal.

The syllabus roughly consisted of making an acquaintance with the machine, computer literacy (type text, try spreadsheet), and a tiny bit of programming with a few instructions. In other words, the grapevine was right – I knew most of it already before class even started. But that did not mean I'd be left to resort to idling in front of the

PC; after all, there is that machine to explore and, all right, *ledigheid is des duivels oorkussen*, or: with not enough assigned tasks to do to remain interested and busy, more or less disruptive fun ensues.

The most fun I had was switching the keyboard cables. I entered the lab early, near the end of the break when there were only a few other students trickling in. I plugged the keyboard and screen cables from our table into the PC of the table next to us, and vice versa. I could see when they typed something and what and then I'd type something else. My classmates sitting at the table next to us, already hesitant with a PC, panicked that their PC had gotten a life of its own. They tried to get the attention of Mr Floppy Disk, who eventually came over to take a look for himself. What our classmates claimed was happening surely was highly improbable. He gave it a try. To his astonishment, the students seemed to be telling the truth. Mr Floppy Disk quickly hit a few keys, but he couldn't figure out what was going on either. He looked as if he thought he was losing it.

'Truly remarkable and odd,' he said. 'One keystroke and another character shows up, and sometimes it seems to be missing a keystroke – and several times there are two different ones!' What oh what could it be?

Linda was leaning to the left to hide behind the monitor because she had started giggling. I was trying very hard to keep a straight face and not turn my head to the right where the teacher was. The longer it went on, the harder it became to not burst out laughing. Eventually neither I nor Linda could hold it in anymore. Mr Floppy Disk glanced at us quizzically.

'What is so funny about it?' he said. Then, when he turned his face to look at us properly, we could see he sensed something was off.

All I could do was point to the cables. The teacher was not happy but I was not punished. Perhaps he could appreciate the prank and acknowledged his foolishness of not double-checking the cabling, but for sure I was filed away as troublemaker. I still duly finished all the exercises that were expected to have been completed that lesson.

The other thing I wasn't supposed to be doing was unplanned and I'd say was not my fault, honestly. I had completed the lesson's exercises and Linda was more than happy that I had, so that she could relax for the hour. We chatted about IT use in the future and speculated about where it would be pervasive.

'Not in my arts and dance,' Linda was convinced, 'so keeping the machine at a distance is fine, really.'

I had started feeling slightly concerned and guilty that I was taking up much more time on the PC than she was. 'It would probably be good to try nonetheless,' I said. 'You never know what the future might bring.'

'Computers and dance? Hah. No way. Besides, we had a deal here. Don't back out of it now,' she responded.

'Okay then,' I mumbled, feeling slightly less concerned.

Even after that conversation, there was still plenty of time left before the end of the lecture hour, so what was one to do? I decided to explore the PC a bit more, to have a look at what other programs were installed on it. This made Linda worry I might break the machine. Unperturbed, I explored further, trying to reassure her that you can't break it with software. I found a list of applications installed, one of which piqued my interest. Its name indicated that it was a calculator for determining the scholarship amount you would receive from the state upon turning 18 and/or enrolling for tertiary education. I was curious. This could be fun, I thought. Wouldn't it be interesting to know, while we continued chatting and fantasising about the future, how much money we'd receive once we were at university studying what we wanted to study?

'Please don't,' Linda said anxiously.

'No worries, it's very true, software cannot ruin the machine,' I told her confidently.

I launched the program and it turned out to be an 80s expert system with an elaborate decision tree that is based on the answers provided to a sequence of questions. It was a type of application I had not tried out yet. The first time I answered the sequence of questions I did them honestly: Yes, I'm 16; Yes, I'm in school …

And so it ended fast with a final message.

System: you will receive 0 guilders.

Meh, but okay, it gave me a sense of the tool's workings: the notion of a decision tree was interesting. We still had time to kill until the end of the class, so I restarted the program and invented a persona so I would be able to see more of the program and, moreover, would be able to figure out what features were the determinants for the final amount of funding. It turned out to be a large decision tree.

When I was somewhere deep down in that tangled tree, Mr Floppy Disk announced that we had to close the programs and shut down the PCs as class was nearly over. But there was no escape from the tree, no menu option with 'exit' or 'quit' or something similarly sensible and useful to have in an application. Linda was getting extremely nervous, and I was starting to worry, slightly, that I might not finish on time. I saw no other option than repeatedly to hit the Enter key many times as fast as I could as a way to arrive at a leaf node.

'You're breaking it!' Linda panicked.

'No, it can't break,' I said. 'It has to stop at some point.'

Indeed it did. Seeing that the screen didn't change anymore as I was hitting the Enter key, there was some relief that it was over. Our classmates had already shut down their PCs and were packing up and standing up to leave. The tiny problem was that last screen, which did not change: it did not have Enter as a possible input key.

System: Printing your scholarship calculations.

Oops!

'Oh, no, please stop!' Here I was again, trying to instruct the computer, but the computer still didn't take voice commands and there was no menu option to cancel it. Even from where we were sitting at the back of the class, I could hear the matrix printer starting with the print job. The deafening noise could be heard over the sound of moving chairs and learners getting up to leave the classroom. Some students exclaimed excitedly with a 'Whoah, something is printing!' Meanwhile I was trying to duck and hide.

'Who the hell sent a print job to the printer?' Mr Floppy Disk shouted. 'That's something you definitely should not have been doing!'

I hesitantly raised my hand.

'Stop it!' he shouted.

'I can't. The program doesn't allow me to,' I squeaked, trying to blame the bad design of the program and apologise at the same time.

Mr Floppy Disk switched off the printer in the middle of the printing job so as to save paper and costly ink. Recognising me from the keyboard incident, he reprimanded me mildly. He told me – which instruction he extended to the rest of the class – that I shouldn't be trying out other programs installed on the PCs. Trying to look remorseful, I promised to watch out for that and be more careful in the future.

I can't recall much else from those IT classes.

....

Many years later, I was the coach of a team of three students who were participating in the world finals of the prestigious International Collegiate Programming Contest. Teams have to solve as many problems as fast as they can on one computer per team, without internet access, and within a set time frame of five hours. The world finals are held each year somewhere in the world, and typically in a fancy hotel that is large enough to house the 120 to 130 teams, coaches, organisers, and sponsors. As coach during the final itself, I didn't have to do much other than make sure the three students in my team were properly dressed, showed up on time at the right places, provide additional psychological support, and socialise with other coaches to exchange notes. We generally had breakfast and dinner together with the team.

At dinner one evening one of the students asked me about my past, although it seemed that all three were curious. Normally students don't ask personal questions, but while these sort of settings are still professional, they are less formal than during lectures and programming contest training days.

'How did you fare in the Olympiad?' one of them enquired, referring to the International Olympiad in

Informatics, which is the main programming contest for teenagers in secondary school. A computer science professor training a team of world-class competitive programmers would obviously have participated in such a contest.

'I didn't,' I replied. 'That is, I never participated. It wasn't a thing back then, at least not at the school that I went to.'

Even if it had been, someone with my track record of class behaviour would not have been selected anyway. It was another round of 'not enough to do' -> 'let's have some fun then' -> 'you definitely will not be given interesting and more challenging tasks'.

I did not quite tell them all those details, but upon their raised eyebrows to my response, I did mention our one-year-IT ('Really only one year, one hour per week?' 'Yes'), the maths cards from primary school (so the Mathematics Olympiad had not been on the cards either), and being last in line for PC access. To their credit, they shook their heads in disbelief: the idea that there could be a system that does not support learners, let alone encourage learners compared to the way they had been encouraged to pursue their interests, was new to them. And PCs with tapes! All so last century. Ancient.

5

BEAUTIFUL BLUE EYES

The Stage: Late 1980s; mid-1990s; early 2010 –
The Netherlands; Peru; South Africa

Are teachers not supposed to stick to their topic and transfer the material impartially to learners and students? Any adult who believes that teachers indeed do so has been indoctrinated adequately and has been sleeping on the job, as it were. Teachers are human too and for sure there's no unbiased neutral teaching going on in the classroom at all times, even when the syllabus is not politics or sociology or the like. Biases and prejudices can shine through to a lesser or greater extent in a multitude of ways.

I gave one example of bias earlier, on the 10-minute talk we had to prepare in Dutch language class, when Johan's long ramble was graded higher than Lucille's clever presentation on the corpus collosum. Unmoderated subjective grades being doled out based on whatever or whomever the teacher prefers was not unusual. There are many more ways to bend things one way or another such that it is – or is not – in a learner's favour. Even classroom layout matters.

Our classes in secondary school were typically a combination of 'sage on the stage' lectures where the teacher talked for a while in front of the class, explaining new material or repeating it yet again, and a more tutorial-like format, where we worked on exercises while the teacher walked around to see how things were going and to explain matters where needed. There were three principal possible configurations of the desks in the class. The 'softer' subjects like languages, history, and geography, saw the one-person desks configured in a smaller U-shape with desks' sides connecting and around the teacher's desk with a larger U-shape behind that with enough space to walk between the two Us, so as to provide seats for about 30 learners. The science subjects of biology, chemistry, and physics were in labs, with larger two-person desks in about four columns of six, with two learners per desk. In mathematics classes, we generally sat in groups of three to four classmates around the tables that were placed together by fours. In Yale's terminology: a double horseshoe with space between the horseshoes, pair pods, and group pods[7], respectively. Positioning of desks affects people's behaviour. There's research about that; I will spice it up with anecdotes.

Let's start with mathematics in group pods. To be sure, all the frustration from primary school 4th grade with those extra exercises cards I had processed in secondary school, and I was enjoying maths again without becoming angry about having been held back. Our teacher was one of those people that make you wonder why they ended up as a school teacher, but otherwise of the mousy, interchangeable variety. Like many Dutch men, he was tall and firmly built, but he also had a short goatee beard, ignoring the impossible to un-think joke by a popular comedian. This same teacher had made harsh comments about a friend with cancer who tried to go back to school just for a few hours per day and had chosen subjects that she considered

---

[7]https://poorvucenter.yale.edu/ClassroomSeatingArrangements (last accessed on 11 May 2021).

useful and enjoyed doing, mathematics among them. Rather than being pleased with the importance my friend placed on mathematics by choosing it, he didn't think it a sensible choice, and he let his opinion be known loud and clear.[8] That made him fall off the default teacher pedestal, among us learners at least; he became someone who joined the ranks of those who are not fully to be trusted.

One day I was in a class of the tutorial variety with this particular mathematics teacher. I had tried all five homework exercises at home already. I was sure I had completed the first four correctly, but I had a question about the fifth. I had made an attempt, but wasn't sure I had done it in the best way possible. The other girls at the table weren't that far yet, so there was no other option but to raise my hand and hope the teacher would grace us with a visit to our table. Thank goodness, eventually, he did. A welcome surprise for a change. He knelt down so as to be at the same height as us sitting on chairs. I wanted to jump into Exercise 5 straight away, but halfway into the long sentence, I was interrupted.

'No, don't jump to Exercise 5,' the teacher said. 'You need to start with the first exercise.'

But I had done the first exercise and I knew it was correct. I had had my hand up for a long time already – it had taken that long for him to come to our table – and could feel myself starting to lose patience.

'I completed exercises 1 to 4 at home,' I told him in the politest way I could muster. 'Those are all clear to me, and the proofs are correct. I have just one question about Exercise 5 –'

---

[8] She died about half a year thereafter, but at that time everyone still had hope that a young person could survive leukaemia against the odds (which turned out to be very bad in the late 1980s), but little did we know. I for sure had no clue and no one bothered to explain it to me (nor, I gather, to many others) and the World Wide Web had yet to be invented.

He ignored me. 'No, let's look at Exercise 1,' he said. And off he went, explaining what I knew I didn't need explained.

'Yes – look here,' I tried, showing him my homework pages. 'I have that answer too. My question is about Exercise 5.'

'No, you have to do them in sequence, so let's have a look at Exercise 2 next.'

I had to endure listening to what I already knew once more. And again, the same ritual – here's my homework, yes, well done, my question is about Exercise 5, no, let's go to Exercise 3. After the explanation of the answer to Exercise 3, I told him in exasperation to please consider my question about Exercise 5, showing him, again, that I had successfully completed exercises 1 to 4 at home.

'Yeah, no, I have already spent so much time at the girls' table with you, you really must try a question yourself now!' he countered. And with that, having been so generous as to have graced our table with a visit, he upped and left for another table, leaving two of my classmates somewhat confused, one shocked at what had just happened, and me livid.

Then came the speculation of trying to make sense of it. We guessed and deliberated several options. Did he start with Exercise 1 regardless because he was convinced we were stupid and lazy, despite the evidence to the contrary? Did he not go to my question about Exercises 5 because secretly he didn't know the answer and he was merely hiding his ignorance? And what the heck was going on in his mind to so blatantly ignore a very clear question? We settled on him being unfit for the job.

I know the maths table I was sitting at wasn't the best table to score on external attributes of nerdiness, even though we'd qualified for the highest level secondary school and our grades had been good enough to select 'the real maths' (*wiskunde B*) and so we would qualify as nerds anywhere else. We were smart girls who also knew how to have a good time. Even among nerds there is a pecking order, however. This was 4th grade, which is when you have started choosing exam subjects, and some self-selection has happened already. It was different in 2nd grade of secondary school, where the HAVO and VWO streams were still mixed. It was the best year of all of the six years at Strabrecht College. I was in the 'waste-basket' class and it was a tremendous amount of fun.

How did I land up in that class? Not by my choice, that's for sure. After the first year of secondary school, the system starts screening bit by bit, and learners are either pushed by their parents to take up Latin and Greek in second year, or they themselves want to do these subjects because they have a knack for languages, or they are discouraged from doing so because they're not good enough. Then there is a fourth possibility: the school 'suggests' to the parents that they force their child to take this option because in the school's estimation their son or daughter dearest is smart and just needs to be challenged a bit more to nudge them onto the nerdy track.

I was classified in that fourth category and was instructed take up that suggestion. Learners were allocated to classes with an optimisation strategy of homogeneity for the first three categories. Then there were the leftovers. That was us.

In our first meet-and-greet lesson at the start of the school year, the head teacher was late so we chatted among ourselves to pass the time. By quick inventory, we estimated that the overflow who actually wanted to do Latin and Greek but weren't in the willing class because of class size limits was about five in number; the ones who didn't want to but were forced to were about 18; and then there were a few recidivists who were ordered to take Latin and Greek along with us. So the vast majority of the class consisted of learners who were smart enough to breeze through school, but had plenty of energy and other interests. Laughter rolled through the classroom in anticipation of a very playful year.

There was a lot of fun to be had, and I have many good memories, as well as the odd not-so-good one. It was a bummer to realise that my contemporaries were as sexist as the Baby Boomer generation (maths class, again! – more about that shortly), and then there was the first of the two blue eyes events – and yet one more instance of a teacher not teaching. It was English class. The teacher, Mr Holt, was a jovial chap who was fun in class, and wasn't convinced that teaching rowdy teenagers was his life's fulfilment. His principal extra-curricular activity was directing the school's annual play, and teaching was more of a means to that end. Arts doesn't pay well in any country. I suppose he was trying to make the best of an unpleasant situation and trying to have an enjoyable time himself. Combine that with a class that preferred to have a good time.

Because we had to put up with Latin and Greek and the system presumed therefore that we should be good in languages, we were allocated only three lessons of English per week rather than the four scheduled for the not-LatinAndGreek stream. I actually needed those four lessons per week, not because I disliked the language – from day one that I had to put up with a lesson in English – but because

I didn't excel in it. I blamed it on the flimsy grammar of the language and not writing what's pronounced – at least for me, those were the two main culprits. The teachers I had throughout the years didn't help me like the language either. The one I had in 3rd grade scored worse (or higher in the demotivational scale) than our play director, but it was the latter who baffled me.[9]

The configuration for English classes was in two U-shapes. I sat in the outer U-shape, somewhere in the middle. It was one of those do-your-own-work sessions, comparable to the maths classes, but instead of the teacher being able to get away with non-randomly going to the various groups of desks, they had to walk by the U-shape in sequence. There was no other way to do it. The only way to avoid a whole subset of the class was to keep hanging around at the end of the U-shape, but that would ignore the 'more deserving' learners along with the somehow undesirables, in case a teacher deemed there were any, so, practically, that was not a viable option.

I can't recall the question I had, but it was a pressing one. I was keeping an eye on Mr Holt to see where he was so I wouldn't miss him when he passed by my desk when progressing through the class. As usual, I had already done the homework at home but still had a question about some part of it that I wanted clarification on. Meanwhile I was having a ball with my classmates sitting nearby while waiting for Mr Holt to come by. Amused, he looked at us and asked rhetorically with a smile on his face, 'Are you having a good time?', which, evidently, we were. But I still had that question.

---

[9]Honestly, I'm not 200% sure it was 2nd and 3rd grade or 3rd and 4th grade, respectively, as our 3rd grade was also still noisier than the average class and I have no written record to verify.

'Yes, thanks,' I said to him. I recall I was also a bit giggly that day as a result of the after-effects of sedation from a visit to the orthodontist; nonetheless, 'I do have a question, though, and was waiting for you.'

He simply laughed that off, that I might actually have a question. Then, staring at me in some amazement, he said: 'Your eyes are very blue.'

Uhm, yes? I indicated, with a nonplussed expression on my face.

'No, I mean, like, really deep blue,' he emphasised. This wasn't quite the response I was expecting to the fact that I had told him I had a question for him. While I was still parsing what he'd said, being somewhat baffled with it, he walked on. My classmates sitting next to me sort of laughed out of awkwardness, and I was left with an unanswered question.

Eventually I caught up on English in Ireland from 1999 onward and it turned out fine, but that's still one of my *what the fuck?!* moments in the process of learning English. Why can't a teacher engage with the question and answer it? How much prejudice exists about girls, giggly girls, or whatever other way non-stereotypical nerdy girls (or boys) behave? How many learners do not have their questions answered? What was that dude thinking waffling about the colour of my eyes instead?

....

Now to that one more bit about maths. We're still in that fun-packed year of second year of secondary school. The mathematics teacher was ill and the class was assigned a substitute. The first female mathematics teacher in the school! The idea was exciting, as in the role model variety and exactly like the STEM promoters claim should happen.

'I studied mathematics, then proceeded to teacher training, and now I'm here and will teach you mathematics for the upcoming months,' she introduced herself.

Brimming with ideals and inexperience, enthusiasm radiated off her. It was good to see that as a girl you could not only enjoy mathematics, but study it and get a degree in it too. Several of us girls in class were impressed. But then came the rest. The offensive was led mainly, I recall, by a nerdy duo and several yay-sayers who bolstered their opinion and boldness.

'It is unacceptable that mathematics is taught by a woman,' one of them said after class. Then, as if the first part of the sentence wasn't clear enough, he added: 'This subject is too important to be taught by a woman.'

'We need to do something about it, to make her go, and then we will be allocated another substitute, which statistically most likely will be a man, as it should be,' the other part of the duo chimed in.

This didn't sound like it was going to end well. There wasn't enough support in class to pester her away, but there was enough support to definitely make it *not* easy to teach our class.

Management intervened. The teacher received support from The System: it was made very clear to us that it was her or no maths and therewith getting behind on the subject. The class chose maths. I still feel sorry for that teacher for what the class did to her – and no one spoke up, not forcefully at least, not even us girls, although some of us did speak up in favour of her. It was a wake-up call. I had assumed the Baby Boomer generation and older were the ones lagging behind in the emancipation of women but that things were better in my generation. They weren't. I realised then that I would likely have to put up with crap from peers if I were to go into STEM. Many years later, a former colleague who had studied mathematics and is only a handful of years older than me, told me that maths was for women too, indeed, and that the percentages were higher than elsewhere in STEM, but that female mathematicians were not-so-subtly directed towards the mathematics teacher specialisation 'since the "real maths" was for men', according to her professors. Perhaps so, too, in the Netherlands – and then still you are thrown to the wolves, who are as unemancipated as their parents.

I should have learned more from that episode. In a roundabout way I ended up in computer science, having worked in IT in a country (Ireland) that was more accommodating to women in IT than the Netherlands, and then in academia in a country (South Africa) that had way more female professors than the Netherlands. So one might be forgiven for thinking things had improved. I am teaching a next generation at the university; surely those students would have made strides towards emancipation and equality.

At one of the universities I taught at, I was allocated the most notorious course of a computer science degree programme: theory of computation. If you want to find a way to sack someone, that's the course to allocate to the colleague. It's challenging to teach and way harder to those enrolled in it. Most students struggle and the average failure rate is much higher than for any other computer science course. First time pass rates of less than 50% are not uncommon and in today's universities, such a pass rate is a waving red flag.

So, when I was teaching it some 10 years ago, there was the regular dissatisfaction. This was compounded by the fact that I was the first female computer scientist that any of the students had encountered in the flesh since they'd started at that university. It had been more than three years since the last woman in computer science at that campus left for some admin job. The lectures were held in typical college hall that can seat about 90 students where rows of seats are positioned in semi-circles of increasing elevation around the lecturer's desk and a blackboard. At the end of a lecture, students then either left or came down to the desk to ask additional questions or questions they hadn't dared to ask in class. At the end of one of my lectures, a whole group descended the steps to where I was standing. They formed a mob of some 15+ students surrounding me in about three-quarters of a circle. They were not physically threatening with fists, but it definitely felt uncomfortable in the sense of possible physical attack on top of their collective attitude. It had me internally preparing physically to stand my ground. Then the verbal pounding that it was all utterly unacceptable began.

'A female teacher for a first-year CS course, meh, possibly acceptable.'

'A female lecturer for a second-year course? No, not really.'

'For a third-year course? Definitely not!'

According to the students, that was, who saw no problem sharing that opinion with me, let alone thinking it in the first place. Checking the exit and the distance thereto, I noticed that some of the other students had decided to hang around in the venue to see how this would end.

I retorted that I had a PhD in computer science and so

was a doctor and thus more than qualified. And that on top of this third-year course I was also teaching an honours (fourth-year) computer science course.

'What?! Utterly unacceptable!' exclaimed a few.

'We will ensure that you are going to be removed from your job.'

'We can't have women teach a core computer science course, let alone honours! It's our future we're talking about!'

They won.

Some of my colleagues were taken aback when I recounted the event, and in a way apologised for it and disapproved of it. 'Yes, that's how they are,' the head of department acquiesced. No backing from higher up, not even from a woman. Whether it was the sexism, racism or xenophobia that weighted in more – tribe over gender – still isn't fully clear to me, and it doesn't matter. What matters is that The System did not support its academics; students' views trump all – even if those views are sexist.

Irrespective of the sour aftertaste of it all, the attitude those students displayed made me recall that second year at secondary school and the female substitute maths teacher. Yet another generation and nothing had changed for the better. The students learned the hard way that it *is* possible to learn something from a female computer scientist, whether they liked it or not. The year thereafter, I worried it would be difficult to find tutors to help in the labs, but in fact it turned out to be remarkably easy; it was even seen as an honour. Later, several of those students seem to have re-evaluated their experience – if wanting to connect via LinkedIn is an indication – yet no one in the whole saga apologised for their sexist ranting, intimidation or support for my ousting that the students were after, or those who supported those trying to push me out. The department has hired five people since I left. All of them are men.

At my former secondary school, there are now three female maths teachers.

And I'm still in the system as well, at a higher ranked university than the one where those students pulled their act. Learners beware: we're hired to teach you, and that may well be more than only the subject matter.

....

The other 'blue eyes' event had nothing to do with teaching, yet was also used as an excuse to not deliver a service. On this occasion the man in question was not a teacher, although it happened during a period I was registered as a student and so you could say that it did teach me something while growing up.

Fast-forward to Peru, 1996, when I was doing my internship for the food science degree from Wageningen, at the *Centro Internacionál de la Papa* (International Potato Centre) (CIP) in Lima, an international research centre that investigates everything about potatoes, from the seeds, plant breeding, growth, harvest, storage, processing into foodstuffs, to nutrition and the economics and sociology of the production column.

The CIP organised the *olympapas*, a sort of olympiad, where different departments competed against one another in various sports. Soccer was only available to the men. We women felt left out, but within CIP there were not nearly enough women in each department, or even across the CIP, to constitute multiple teams. The solution proposed was for the women to team up into one large team and play against the women's soccer team of the agricultural university across the road. They had won the nationals the year before, so it was extremely unlikely that we would win – a good way to teach the noisy international women a lesson. It was intimidating indeed, but having insisted on playing soccer too, we couldn't back down. We decided to practise in the hope we would not be a total walk-over in the anticipated friendly match. Those practices were joyful, with a mix of people, including Peruvians who wanted to try out soccer or finally saw their chance to play beyond the informal attempts at home, enthusiasts from abroad (myself included), and from any role in the organisation across hierarchies. A few men were willing or had, tongue-in-cheek, 'sacrificed' their time to try to teach us. It was springtime with lovely late-afternoon sunshine at the end of the workdays to run around on the concrete sports field on the CIP's premises.

At one of the practice sessions where I was left forward, I looked behind me to check if there was someone from the other team nearby. If there was, I would have to kick the ball in the direction of the goal straight away; if there wasn't, I could dribble to the goal so as to not risk missing. There was no one, so I wanted to start dribbling with the other foot, but instead of putting my foot down next to the ball, I put it on the ball, yet shifted my weight onto the other side nonetheless. I fell, with my side and leg hitting the concrete but my foot still on the ball, which couldn't roll away because my other foot had kept it in place. It hurt! A scream followed near-instantly, and a few colleagues came onto the field to see how badly I was hurt.

My foot was hanging limp and at a bit of an odd angle. The only part I could move, and only slightly, was my big toe. Every movement sent a shockwave of pain through it. I was assisted to the side and someone got some ice to put on the ankle, and we were all hoping it was just a minor sprain.

By the next day it hadn't improved much and eventually I went to the hospital to have it checked out, as the CIP doctor was concerned. They confirmed nothing was broken, but it was *esquince en el tercer grado*, or 'third degree sprained'. I learned a lot of new Spanish vocabulary and some human anatomy: in spraining, first you stretch the ligaments, then you stretch the tendon, then you tear the ligaments, and then you tear the tendon, finally you break the ligaments, and then as final stage you break the tendon. My peroneal tendon was, according to the doctor, about 99% torn – 100% would have meant an operation. The sliver of connection merited a cast around the foot, in the hope that the tendon would grow back. With no other choice, a cast it was.

Afterwards, I called my health insurance in the Netherlands, on an expensive international phone call. I explained the situation and diagnosis.

'That is unfortunate indeed. They should have stitched the pieces of tendon together in the hospital, not merely put the foot in a cast' was the first not-so-reassuring response of the insurance lady at the other end of the line.

'And now?' I asked. 'Do I have to go back to the Netherlands for that? I have another one and a half months here in Peru to finish my research project.' I was flip-flopping a bit on wanting good health care and wanting to stay until the planned end of the project.

'No,' she responded, 'we can't do anything for you now,

because that stitching together should happen within 72 hours and anyway it is not life threatening so not worth it to repatriate you all the way from Peru.'

The concept of 'reduced quality of life due to limited services' either wasn't operational then or I was already bucketed into the 'not economically active, so low priority' category that I was explicitly categorised in later when I returned to the Netherlands. Anyway, since there was no other choice, it was a case of hoping for the best.

After some weeks, it was time to remove the cast. Ignoramus that I was, I asked the doctor about the next step, which I assumed to be physiotherapy, since other people I knew of who'd had casts around limbs removed, moved on to physio to regain and strengthen function. I wanted to return to playing soccer at CIP and go out and dance again now that I had managed to grasp the basics of salsa dance, among many things. I had practised saying this in my best Spanish, including verifying the words in the dictionary and the verb conjugation in the grammar book.

'No, no physiotherapy,' was the doctor's response.

He looked to be in his 60s and ready for retirement, so I was wondering that maybe he had forgotten his youth or didn't grasp that I was young still and wanted to do lots of things fast, including sports. So I tried again, in different wording and mentioning the soccer and sports more generally.

His response to me, in unambiguous Spanish and spoken with a reassuring tone, was: 'Don't worry. You have beautiful blue eyes. You will get a husband and children.'

'But I want to play soccer now?!'

'*No te preoccupes* ...' (don't worry ...)

Nearly 25 years later, it's no soccer, no husband, and no children. Of the 'among many things', dancing was what I missed most. I learned things I didn't think I was interested in – computer science among them – and things I didn't even knew existed back then. I met people I'm glad to have met, have done some awesome travels and other activities, and my life turned out in a different way than I had planned and isn't all that bad now. Still, I'd have much preferred it if more sensible post-cast care had paved the way towards a return to a fully functional ankle, to not have had to be a participant in some second-rate health care intervention.

A sexist teaching event can be conquered or avoided by switching tracks, but a physical limitation is something one has to learn to live with daily for the rest of one's life, even when experienced through beautiful blue eyes.

6

A SMART GIRL IS PREPARED FOR HER FUTURE

The Stage: Early 1990s – The Netherlands;
many countries too

Een slimme meid is op haar toekomst voorbereid (a smart girl is prepared for her future).

This was the state's slogan of a campaign to prod girls to study a degree in Science, Technology, Engineering, or Mathematics (STEM). From a language viewpoint, it does rhyme; from any other viewpoint, it doesn't quite add up. Within the parameters given, women born in 1972 or later are screwed, no matter what. But there is a way out, for some of us at least, and there might be a utopia in Rutger Bregman's sense of the 'utopia for realists' as a solution for more women and some men. The latter, however, is going to require a revolution of sorts to realise it.

But let's not get ahead of ourselves. Let's start with that slogan and where it came from. What was its purpose, short term and long term? How could and/or would it affect me and my contemporaries? To answer these questions, we need to take a few steps back in time, starting with the welfare state's pension system and its assumptions when it was conceived, as I did in my teens when all this was playing out. I pieced the case together mainly from the regional daily newspaper, *Eindhovens Dagblad*, two weeklies (*De Tijd* and *Intermediair*) and the TV and radio news. The topic was also discussed at secondary school in sociology classes, on top of the background knowledge of Dutch society.

The make-up of the typical population of a country is pyramid shaped, that is, young people in the majority at the bottom and fewer elderly above them. This means that there are many more people of working age who can contribute to the 7-12 years, on average, a pensioner lives off a pension. So that made sense at the time. It was clear and simple then. The husband of the nuclear family works, his wife stays home to raise the kids, and when he retires at 65, they receive a monthly pension from the state. When he dies at the life expectancy for men at the time, 72, the widow keeps living off his pension; widow of said deceased husband, statistically, will die at 77.

There are several problems with this scheme, of which two are relevant here. If the wife had had more than enough of her husband and she'd divorced him, she would not receive a share in the pension, since the pension was in her ex-husband's name and it was his number of years of work that mattered. This financial stranglehold for old age was deemed unfair. To boot, if I remember correctly, it did not work for the rare case of the other way around, that is, the wife works but the stay-at-home husband would not live off her pension. Moreover, this state of affairs did not treat women and men as equals before the law. That was deemed unfair as well, in feminist circles in the Netherlands at least, and had to change.

There was another issue that was spoken less about, but that forward-looking bean counters had noticed with some initial concerns and was noted on the side occasionally: those post-World War II Baby Boomers weren't popping out as many offspring as previous generations. This messed up the pyramid scheme of population make-up into something more resembling an onion. If those Baby Boomers were to retire *en masse*, there would not be enough people in the workforce paying taxes to pay for their basic pension. In addition, if they were to live longer than statistically they were supposed to, it would put an even greater strain on the pension system. By the late 1980s it was clear that the pension systems in place in most of the West were going to run into serious problems. This triad of issues with their adherents resulted in an odd alliance to come to the solution to kill many birds with one stone. The feminists' excitement radiated through their voices on the radio and TV news bulletins.

First: the feminists would have it their way and men and women would become truly equal before the law. The bean counters patted themselves on the back for appearing emancipated and supporting this request. They asked the feminists whether they truly realised what they were asking for: there would be no leaning on or chaining themselves to husbands; women would have to work for their pension, much the same as men already did. 'Giving up a comfortable situation for ideals? Are you sure?' 'Yes,' the so-called second-wave feminists reiterated, 'and it's not all that comfortable to everyone.'

Second: this meant that women had to be prodded to go to work, thereby increasing the working population that pays taxes to sustain the pension system; and *voilà*, there's the boon for the bean counters who were looking at creating a chance to balance future budgets.

Third: it would be good if the girls and young women succeeded in obtaining decent-paying jobs. Traditional 'women's jobs', such as nursing, teaching, and secretarial work, don't come with generous wages. Hence, they shouldn't study for such professions that either pay little or, not infrequently, lead to unemployment, but rather for professions for which there is ample work. Not only that, but especially for the kind of jobs that pay well, because you might have to factor in that you're out of the running for a few years when raising children, where you'd have to patch up that gap in pension build-up. Those feminists who were nagging to have that pure equality? Well, you'll darn well have to work extra hard for it then or stop breeding and build up that pension well.

Such explanations made the whole plan smell fishy and, frankly, it was somewhat confusing when I was reading the news articles about it. Were they actually saying that with that new law, we'd be worse off in our pensionable age, no matter what? If we popped out many babies, then there would be enough people of working age to pay for our pensions ... but then we would not receive that money because we wouldn't be able to hitchhike along with our partner anymore. Or ask your partner nicely and stay with them until the end ... but then we're back at square one again.

If we popped out a few babies as a middle-of-the road strategy, there would still either be a 'baby gap' in the build-up of pensionable years for a few years at least (and so less pension money), or live with the scorn of full-time working mum leaving the kids alone instead of fulfilling the wifely and motherly duties more comprehensively.

If we didn't pop out any babies at all, we'd be able to

save the same amount as men (if we had equal pay) but then there would be even fewer people to pay for our pensions, which would not be good for The System either. It doesn't matter what you do; the prospects are not good. I wasn't convinced. I wanted equality, sure, but this didn't quite sound like equality either.

Anyhow, what are the professions with good salaries? Those in science, technology, and engineering. So, if you're smart about planning your future, and know about the consequences of total equality before the law, then you'd better prepare adequately and choose a degree in STEM instead of some frivolous one that is likely to lead to unemployment. Or so went the public education campaign. They could not factor in those women who were housewives already, since they'd be unprepared, so the focus needed to be girls with their future ahead of them – girls who would turn 18 in 1990 or later.

I turned 18 in 1991. The state-sponsored citizen education programme was for me and my classmates, who were about to choose a degree. There were TV spots and posters with girls saying they were doing the smart thing by choosing a STEM field. This chapter's title refers to the slogan that was supposed to make us choose a STEM degree, 'a smart girl is prepared for her future'. The 'logic' that ensued in discussions about it were alike: 'Ah, and so then if you don't choose a STEM degree, then you're not smart. Just so you know', the intention being to push you into a STEM degree and, *en passant*, annoy girls who preferred a non-STEM degree programme. Or you'd be ill-prepared for a future that was another 40 years away, which is a very long time away when you're 17 or 18 and have to choose a degree. True, you'd be less worse off than if you'd married a lousy husband you'd need to divorce, but no one in their teens assumes they're going to marry a bastard – that statistic applies to other people. Hence, worse off it would be then, it seemed.

To me and some other 10-15% of girls, it didn't make a difference, because we were already interested in the STEM fields anyway and did not need any convincing and I cannot recall any of my classmates being swayed by the campaign either. The *flutstudies* (lousy degrees), supposedly to become a highly educated housewife and candidate for part-time work, were still heavily subscribed.

....

A stocktaking after 30 years showed that the campaign did have an effect: so-called 'economic independence' of women went up from 25% to 65%, albeit mostly with part-time work and lower pay. That 'economically independent' is a bit of a misnomer by the Dutch Statistics office, since according to their definition, it means that then you earn at least 70% of the minimum wage.[10] The meaning of minimum wage, officially, is the lowest amount that employers can legally pay their employees, but that is based on the understanding that that amount, when working full-time, suffices to be economically independent in the sense of being able to survive on it. In the Netherlands, in line with the notion that women earn less for the same work, as is the case almost everywhere else in the world, a lesser amount would be applicable to minimum wage, too, apparently. Not officially for the law, of course not – just for serving up shiny statistics.

---

[10]https://www.rtlnieuws.nl/nieuws/nederland/artikel/4927036/vrouwen-werk-economisch-zelfstandig-moeders-gezin-emancipatie (last accessed on 20 Feb 2021).

To the best of my knowledge, the Netherlands was the only European country that had what was called 'the full 100% equality', at the time at least. Now we had to work, or work more, in better-paying jobs, and if we were to take time out for childbirth and tending to toddlers for a few years, let alone be a stay-at-home mom for our children's whole youth, we would receive a somewhat to substantially lower pension by the time we retired than if we had worked all the time. Also, upon retirement, one cannot lean on the husband anymore for a pension, because it's the woman's own responsibility. So, it looks a lot like having to work substantially harder for much lower pension payments. On the flip side, divorce has less dire financial ramifications.

And so, is this smart woman prepared for her future? I tick all the boxes they had foreseen in the 1980s, but there are a few kinks. One of these – and this counts for anyone in the same boat, not only for women – relates to moving abroad to work in another European Union country at a time when there is no European pension system; another is changing companies rather than building up a pension with one employer. This sort of patchwork of employment is certainly not atypical and it's also not good for one's pension saving plans. For instance, if I were to return to the Netherlands, they'd see I have not been duly paying taxes there (I did, and still do, in the countries where I work(ed)), so that would be the minimum pension benefit to scrape by at best (if at all), and collecting a few cents from each past employer and country might cost more money than that it would gain. So, a suitably prepared lass still isn't quite prepared for that future.

Second, even if there's no 'baby gap' in a woman's employment record, there's the issue of temping, being paid less than a man for the same job, and delayed promotions, all of which contribute to lower pension savings than men amass on average. This is not intended as a whining exercise. I am setting down simple facts and statistics – and these I can spice up with plenty of anecdotes.

About 80% of income of a male colleague? Check (my stint at Compaq, at least).

Temping rather than tenure? Check (see Chapter 13 for some juicy details).

Delayed promotion? Check (see Chapter 14).

What to do? Be sure to reside in a country where euthanasia is legal, so that you can end it when you want to and die with dignity, rather than ending up being 70+ living under a bridge. Or marry a rich significant other – man or woman, whatever floats your boat, as long as the nation's laws say you can get your hands on their money after they die. It's not unlike the 'back to start' card in Monopoly: no real advance made in the end after all. Not only no real advance: women now also have to work and pay for the current pensioners, which benefits the current pensioners, who are, perhaps not so incidentally, those who proposed the 'true equality' in the first place.

....

Are the only options in effect nothing but lose-lose or trying to go for 'emulating the traditional man's job and career trajectory' in an attempt to secure a decent pension? First, pension is not everything: many people die before retirement anyway and so may you or I. Second, depending on the country you live, there may be the concept of ubuntu or the custom of paying 'black tax', with the net effect that your children and/or grandchildren contribute directly to your living expenses in old age. Third, go for a so-called 'joint-outside option', to borrow a term from game theory: a gentle revolution of sorts, where pension pay-outs do not depend on how much you have contributed to the economy in terms of the capitalist bean counting. It can easily be part of a universal basic income programme. That can be a way to achieve equality, one without penalising whoever takes care of the children.

PART TWO

SEARCHING FOR GREEN PASTURES

7

PROGRESSIVE STUDENTS, UNITE

The Stage: 1990s – The Netherlands;
University City

In early August 1992, at long last, I could run off to university and rent the attic in a house and call that whole room all mine. There was also a small kitchen with a carpet on the floor, that turned sticky after a while, which I shared with a first-year student who rented a room on the first floor of the house. She, too, went on to obtain a PhD and proceeded to an international career, but in wastewater treatment in industry. The other sizeable room on the first floor was rented out initially to a male student in agricultural economics and later to varying numbers of Somalian refugees; the small extra room was eventually also rented out, to a young Somali woman. The retired granny landlady lived on the ground floor; she could no longer walk up the stairs so we had free rein upstairs. We had loads of energy and were excited about our turn to create the future.

We were at the right place, it seemed. Wageningen was a university town full of world-improvers, or at least with aspirations thereto. The university's buildings were scattered around the town, which is located in the centre of the country and about 80 kilometres up north from Heeze.

It was undoubtedly a city, in my opinion, irrespective of some medieval piece of paper giving it city rights: it had a movie house and a swimming pool, which, to my mind, were the necessary and sufficient criteria. I expected that the difference of less-oppressive *milieux* between primary and secondary school would be one of a major jump to open-mindedness at the university and beyond. I was looking forward to that. At university I'd get to learn more about the coolest subjects the whole time, rather than have to spend time on subjects I found boring, like English or Dutch language and literature. At university there wouldn't be any sexism because surely everyone would be smart. At university, and living independent student life, I'd finally be the adult I was already by age, with my own budget and choices to make. A new chapter in life, full of possibilities, opportunities to create and take, and boundaries to push to explore the world further.

The special slice of the world in Wageningen resembled a socialist and environmentalist enclave surrounded by hardcore, narrow-minded Protestant conservatism. There were a few anachronisms that spilled over from those surroundings. Neighbouring town Ede had a sizeable adult population that voted for a certain political party (the SGP), which only in 2010 was ordered by the Dutch supreme court to allow women to stand for election, which decision was upheld in the European Court of Human Rights. Yes, the SGP disagreed so much with the idea that women should be allowed to be elected that they fought the court's decision all the way to the European Union level – and lost resoundingly there as well. That sort of Protestant fundamentalism does exist in the Netherlands and the fundamentalists actually do send their offspring to university, even to study evolution-drenched degrees like plant breeding. At times such diversity made for lively debates and jokes.

Setting aside those surroundings for a moment, it appeared there was some curiosity regarding the degree I had enrolled in. This became readily apparent in the third trimester when we attended our first degree-specific course. *Levensmiddelentechnologie* is variously translated as food science, food technology, or food engineering, but either way it is definitely not to be confused with *Voeding* (human nutrition). The former has the product as central focus and the latter has the human as its focus. It looks at how to produce that edible product. For instance, how to scale up baking bread in a factory (not one loaf at a time), invent new products or the same produce with novel ingredients (for example, mycoprotein-based meat alternatives, at that time, and, more recently, 'insect milk'-based ice- cream[11]), and ensure that when producing and transporting the food, it won't contain harmful moulds and bacteria or their toxins by the time you obtain it. This requires an interdisciplinary background that of itself has become a unique approach and discipline. For instance, physicists and mechanical engineers invented the microwave, very true, but they could not have foreseen, nor explained, why eggs explode in the microwave[12] (you can try this experiment at home, provided you clean it up yourself). Physical chemistry offers rheology but that alone doesn't solve the problem of trying to wrangle a

---

[11]More precisely, the EntoMilk is made from black soldier fly larvae; more information: https://gourmetgrubb.com/entomilk/ (last checked on 4 September 2021). It is a newer invention than what we were exposed to during the degree in the 1990s. The mycoprotein was of those times.

[12]For the curious: the deformation of the protein structures in the egg white makes it take up more space (from coiled up to somewhat straight), and therewith expanding in size. The shell expands, too, but not as fast as the egg white does. And voilà, the exploding egg.

steady stream of ketchup out of the bottle.[13] Biologists have a taxonomy for plants, but that doesn't resolve how to keep the vegetables clean, packaged, and fresh for consumption[14], to name but a few examples of problems that are on a food technologist's plate.

Since food science had as prerequisites mathematics, physics, chemistry, and actually biology too, I had expected to be in a minority, as STEM wasn't popular with girls at secondary school. It turned out there was a whopping 60-70% women in our cohort. We were all surprised by that and we wanted to know ourselves how that had happened, since chemistry degree programmes, for example, had barely 5% women. The older brother of a friend was in the chemistry degree programme at the nearby university in Eindhoven, where there were three women and some 500 men in their cohort. We all knew about such data and wanted to compare notes to figure out this anomaly beyond our own assumption and anecdote, or statistical anomaly, if you prefer.

At a brief lunch with around eight classmates in the Biotechnion's cafeteria on the *Wageningse berg* (Wageningen mountain – geographically a misnomer but it required non-trivial cycling uphill to go to class, so it sure felt like a mountain) between morning lectures and the afternoon practical work in the lab, the topic came up. I mentioned my reasoning and meandering, and how my wanting to combine chemistry and biology had led me to stumble upon food science when I was looking for a degree that offered these.

---

[13]Different layers of molecules have to roll over each other steadily, not become tangled and then swoosh all in one go because of too much pressure build-up.
[14]There's a nice kitchen experiment with tomatoes and ripening bananas, thanks to the molecule ethylene (C_2H_4). Or you could try to find out why any vegetable from a tin can does not nearly taste like fresh produce.

'Yes, me too,' came several responses from other female students.

'Me too,' said another, 'but I wanted to combine physics and chemistry.'

A few other students had been nudged or directed into 'something more applied that would be good for them'.

'I had worried that I might not be cut out for the physics/chemistry degree, that it would be too hard to do,' someone else added, 'because the professors presented themselves as playing hardball at the open days and visits.'

A further few admitted softly: 'Yeah, that too, if I have to be honest.'

But, we all agreed, this degree wasn't any less challenging or easier, it was only less threatening. We were young women who had a final mark of typically 7 or 8 on a scale of 10 on those exam subjects, when a 5.5 would have gotten you accepted into either degree programme. That career adviser and the chemistry teacher crossed my mind. We resolved to raise the questions unobtrusively with staff as well, to see whether they had any explanation. One of the food science professors mentioned that several years earlier, it was still the other way around, with many more men than women enrolled, but that it had gradually been changing. They had no idea why. It certainly was not thanks to some outreach activities, they admitted, since such activities were non-existent, and the numbers had already been going up before the 'smart girl' campaign.

Practically, it meant that we could safely be invited to any study-specific party without messing up the gender balance. This in contrast to, among others, animal husbandry (mostly men) and nutrition (mostly women), although across the university it was fairly evenly spread, so that there were always workable combinations for a joint party so that anyone who wanted could have a fair chance to score on the meat market.

All degrees from Wageningen University (except one or two) are in engineering so that it earned you the protected title *ingenieur*, 'Ir', as is the case with the degrees of the three technical universities in the Netherlands, yet curiously with a gender balance that wasn't even attempted as recruitment strategy.

There were mathematics courses as well. In the first trimester, we had to take a course in mathematics covering topics such as integrals, differential equations, matrices, vectors and functions at a more advanced level than we'd done at secondary school. The course went smoothly. In the second trimester we had to take a course in statistics, with the different statistical tests in the context of scientific experiments in agriculture. That went smoothly too. Mathematics was applied throughout the courses in the degree programme in a wide range of subjects. That also went smoothly. I cannot recall one single instance on the maths front even vaguely resembling those from primary and secondary school. There were many decent people with their hearts and minds in the right place.

It was a little like a brave new world or a microcosm of a possible future society. We were young, hungry for knowledge and skills, and full of ideals – equality being one of them. We were determined to realise our ideals to improve the lot for our generation and for those to come.

....

There was an occasional cloud in the sky indicating

that all may not be that wonderful out there in the real world and that, maybe, we might have to adjust to the old guard after graduation. Two clouds were in connection with activities when I was member of the *Progressieve Studentenfraktie* (PSF) (Progressive Student Party) and had a seat at the table for adults.

It was a real seat. Once upon a time, there was a democratic university that was governed by all citizens of Academistan: academics, support staff, students, and elders or people from industry. Since the Agricultural University in Wageningen was a small university intentionally consisting of only one faculty, the typical governance structures of faculty councils, university council, and senate were all rolled into one entity, the *universiteitsraad*. The *raad* was made up of 14 academics, seven support staff, seven students and, if I remember correctly, five members from outside the university who held senior position there (or maybe three; I remember only two). Each member had one vote. The academics and the students had political parties in a progressives and conservatives/ religious divide. I was one of the elected student members of the progressive party (PSF). We had to decide on topics such as the reorganisation of the university's management structures, the budget, degree programmes, buildings, student affairs and so on.

The two female outside-university members were awesome. Dr Goedmakers was of the feisty feminist variety and Ir Augustijn van Buuren looked friendly and granny-like but most certainly was a feminist as well. Both were successful professionals already back then in the mid-1990s and continued to be so afterwards. They were well-groomed, persuasive speakers, and when either of them said something during the meetings, everyone listened. It was good to see that it was possible to make it outside the university in the agricultural sector.

During one of our 'chatting about the other council members' interludes after one of the weekly party meetings in the sun parlour of the historical building of the Wageningen Student Organisation, we were in agreement that in all likelihood it must have been far from easy to have a successful career in a man's world.

'You almost can see from their appearance that they have weathered storms,' one of the party members said.

'Would it have been different numbers of obstacles they have overcome or might it have been different attitudes of how you deal with them that made them each end up with a different approach?' asked another to no one in particular, depositing the question in the group. All five of us wondered and pondered for a while, without coming to a conclusive answer. Sitting on the other side now, I think it was probably a combination.

The third woman of note in the *universiteitsraad* was the conservative academics party member Dr Rietjens – if there was a STEM academic role model for any of us female students in the PSF and related student union, it was her. Or else Dr Fresco, if you were more on the plant breeding side of agriculture. Dr Rietjens had an excellent research track record in toxicology, was a good teacher – well, at least the times I sat in her lectures she was, and I don't recall negative gossip about her teaching – and took on those additional activities such as the active membership of the *universiteitsraad*. And she was well spoken and well groomed on top of it. Well spoken was, perhaps, not a requirement for male professors – well groomed most certainly was not. A professor position had become available in the Toxicology department. Dr Rietjens was a perfect fit and everyone assumed she'd be awarded the position.

She wasn't.

It was such a shock to everyone that there was a public outcry and demands for an inquiry. Surely the only reason could be a bunch of sexist professors on the selection committee? The selection committee shielded itself behind the customary confidentiality of the appointment processes, and so the outcry was to no avail. She became a full professor eventually. Looking up the easy data on Google Scholar in late 2020, I found a very impressive track record indeed, with nearly 19 000 citations and an h-index of 70 (meaning at least 70 of her scientific papers have each been cited at least 70 times in other scientific papers – that's a lot). Back then it did make me wonder just how many more 'more achievements' women had to have on their CVs to be considered equally suitable for a job. Now I know the answer: a *lot* more.

With that going on, around the same time there were interviews and public guest lectures for other professorial appointments, and, as PSF members, occasionally we were invited to sit in to form an opinion ourselves, in case there was more nonsense – this because the *universiteitsraad* had to formally approve professorial appointments. Even if we could not block a proposed appointment with the votes of our party alone, at least we'd be able ruffle the feathers and keep the system on its toes, and everyone knew that.

As part of that involvement, we were able to obtain statistics of female professors in the Netherlands as compared to the rest of the world. Based on the data from the early 1990s, the Netherlands was in the bottom five of the ranking of pretty much all countries in the world, along with countries such as Pakistan, Bangladesh, and Saudi Arabia, with about 5% female professors. Something was seriously amiss. Those countries were portrayed as rather backward on the emancipation of women, and there the Netherlands was, keeping them company.

We didn't really understand how it could have been this bad. After all, there didn't seem to be that much sexism? Admittedly, you were more likely to see the imbalance at the technical universities, and if you start out with few women in an undergraduate degree programme, then the pool to choose from post-PhD is even smaller. This was the prevailing assumption and explanation. There were occasional further attempts to explain it away with assertions that girls simply weren't interested in technology and academia, as if there had been a survey – representative or otherwise – that said so. Even if there had been a survey that said so, would it not have been different at the general universities and should this not have pushed up the national percentage? Moreover, weren't universities enlightened spaces with intelligent people who surely would grasp the notion of equality? Even with this dire data in hand, we dismissed the Toxicology hiring committee's act as an aberration that managed to fall through the cracks of The System, since no other such incidents had hit the news. And news was news – reported with [Protestant/Catholic/ Humanist] and [Left/Centre/Right] rosy glasses on, but not messed up with fake news or suffering from omitted newsworthy items. 'Pravda news' sort of news was something of dictatorships next door in Eastern Europe.

For the record, we were not as naive as all this may

sound now. We were merely more familiar with the sexism the way it happened in the places where we had grown up. For both of us (the other woman PSF member and me), less sexism during our studies and extra-curricular activities felt in the order of a step forward already. As for the men in the PSF, they had a few gratuitous extra lessons on feminism when these were deemed necessary, which would have opened their eyes in case they had been closed and which had them re-evaluating their youth. Further, there were more women at the university at the time, including enrolled in PhD programmes, than 10-20 years before – the time it would otherwise have taken for those female students from around 1980 to rise in the ranks. According to the anecdata, things were changing. Our time was coming.

....

Let's hit the fast-forward button a generous 15 years for a new stocktaking. It was nearing 12% according to the 2009 report from Sofokles. Apparently, our time still had to come. Fast-forward another 10 years: it reached around 23% in 2019, with the note that in 2016 the Netherlands had earned itself 24th place out of the 28 EU countries (it was still 18.7% then). Wageningen is not the worst off with its current 16.9% female professors[15], and it is more than double the last number I can remember (7.8%), and in the same range as the technical universities. Yet, would those 83.1% male professors in engineering never contemplate that something just might be slightly amiss with the fact that there are few female colleagues indeed, even though

[15]https://www.lnvh.nl/monitor2019/ (last checked on 4 September 2021).

half of the students are female? Hint: it's neither for lack of competencies nor of ambition.[16]

A 20% increase in female professors nationally over roughly 25 years – a whole generation – is quite a glacial pace. Plenty of women do obtain PhDs, but there are leaking pipelines, glass ceilings, and men-only elevators. Not that all this discouraged me from staying in agriculture (there were other pastures, which are to be continued in Chapter 9). Perhaps I should have let all the data sink in better, but I chose instead to pursue my interests regardless, come what may.

---

[16]There have been many scientific articles over the years across disciplines and countries, including evaluations for hiring, promotion, and funding, conducted with controlled artificial set-ups or real-world data. A trend-setting early study was: Steinpreis, R.E., Anders, K.A. and Ritzke, D. The impact of gender on the review of the curricula vitae of job applicants and tenure candidates: A national empirical study. Sex roles, 1999, 41(7): pp 509–528. A recent example from France: Régner, I., Thinus-Blanc, C., Netter, A., Schmader, T. and Huguet, P. Committees with implicit biases promote fewer women when they do not believe gender bias exists. Nature human behaviour, 2019, 3(11), 1171–1179.

8

LET THE MEN DO THE HEAVY WORK

The Stage: Mid-1990s – Lima, Peru;
elsewhere too

'I have this broken TL lamp in the kitchen that I haven't figured out yet how to fix,' I strategically mentioned to a neighbour who lives down the road. I hadn't had time to look at it, but he felt down and dumb after hearing I was employed as a prof and he enjoys being the handyman in the street. He knew how to remove the TL lights, which wasn't easy to do, and he felt his importance was restored again. Wonderfully, he even went out and bought two new lights for me and all was well.

Or was it?

I would not have exploited the opportunity – an *un*-feminist thing to do by Dutch standards – had I not learned a thing or two in Peru. Let's rewind to that 6.5-month stint as visiting student researcher in 1996.

Wageningen University being world renowned in agriculture, we could choose wherever we wanted to go to do our stage, that is, professional work or research experience outside the university for between three months up to a year. My first choice was Peru. I had researched the country in 6th grade in primary school for a geography essay on climate zones (it had five at the time, not the boring one in the Netherlands) and they speak Spanish there (most beautiful language that I know) and there's lots of history and culture to explore (a nice bonus). I asked around in the Food Science department and, yes, one prof, Dr Nout, had a contact in Peru in food science, which I was still studying at the time. She was employed as temping researcher at the CIP in Lima as overseas development assistance. It was a contact in food processing rather than in the bioconversions that I was specialising in[17], but perhaps things could be stretched and nudged and learned fast to fit in their scope?

Sure they could, and off I went in June 1996 for my second intercontinental trip. I had attended barely a handful of Spanish lessons, but brought the textbooks and a dictionary and hoped for the best to learn it there. I had also completed a short course on 'Living and working in a different culture'. Some joking *baraksgenoten* (flatmates – the student flat being an asbestos-lined wooden barrack) had given me as a farewell gift a few of those Bouquet booklets about finding love the old-fashioned way. Those short love stories about a nurse falling for the tall, dark, and handsome doctor and a young working woman being swept off her feet by a brusque, blue-eyed baron with his heart in the right place. This way, my flatmates surmised, I would finally learn how to behave as a submissive lady and second-class human, since assumptions were that Latin America was rather behind in emancipation, let alone cognisant of feminism.

---

[17]Fermentation with microbes and biochemistry with enzymes and such, as in beer, wine, bread, yoghurt, cheese, bioplastics from white rot fungi, detoxifying cassava and apricot seeds, and colouring pale salmon with pink colour-producing bacteria added to the water, to name but a few processes, products, and applications.

As it turned out, it was a mix: some people were well aware of feminism and went for it, some tried to ignore it, and others were actively against it.

First came the 'survival skills for women' offered by international scientists during a break from work at a CIP office. According to one of them, sighing on the topic, 'It is a lot better here compared to the machismo in Mexico. If you can't handle it here, then definitely don't go there,' was her advice. 'Here, it feels like taking a bit of a break and I'm glad to just be able to breathe again.'

'I've taken a boyfriend for convenience, and I suggest you do the same,' offered another, which suggestion drew a grimace and a questioning look from me. 'A woman alone, especially an international one, is a target, but with a boyfriend you're harassed less and can go out more,' she explained.

'Isn't that a bit morally dubious and somewhat unfair to your boyfriend?' I asked.

'Yes,' she said, 'and I do feel a bit guilty, but society is also a bit to blame.'

The researcher who was my internship contact had tried the boyfriend route but it didn't work out; she blamed everything and everybody for things not going as smoothly as they did back home, where she could buy her type of clothes, eat ecologically responsibly, have an asymmetric haircut, and where *mañana* indeed does mean it will happen tomorrow.

Overall, the three experiences did not help much. I would have to discover the country and decide for myself what the story was with men there. The first step was to try to learn Spanish very quickly in order to be able to have at least half of a basic conversation to be able to socialise.

Next, I dyed my hair black. I had long blonde hair and couldn't cross the street in peace and quiet. It was nice to be noticed, sure, but it was enough already. The black hair experiment was a total failure aesthetically (brown worked better), but after that I was bothered less often and did not have cars using their horn every other minute when they passed by when I walked on the pavement along Avenida Sucre in the Pueblo Libre quarter of Lima. I almost appreciated that I wasn't gorgeous according to some standard. Men still started random conversations often, but, as time progressed, and the combination of clothes-destroying all-purpose washing powder and a severe water shortage made me have to buy some local clothes, I was left to my own devices more.

Clothes are funny things. The ones I brought with me from the Netherlands were 'decent' in that they were neither too sexy and revealing nor conservative long-sleeved baggy clothes to hide yourself in. Women's clothing on sale in Lima was definitely in the 'sexy' and 'revealing' category by Dutch standards, such as tight or cropped T-shirts where the navel is exposed or slightly see-through lace blouses. There was no other option than to buy and wear them, no matter the feeling of nakedness. The first time I wore a lace blouse and walked out to the supermarket, men didn't ogle nearly as much as they had before. They were used to see woman 'half naked', so that when I dressed myself in what were definitely sexier clothes, I was simply blending into the masses.

I was to learn more about clothes, well beyond what is practical for an agronomist in the field. In the workplace, more specifically – policed and judged we were then and still are now.

A side-effect with the clothes I bought in Peru was that I was starting to look mainstream, resembling other young women there. One day at the CIP, out of the blue, I started receiving compliments about my attire, for having the good taste to adjust to Peru and being properly dressed now. 'Not like the temp researcher,' a colleague added on the off-chance that the first compliment might have been lost in translation, which it wasn't.

'And being properly dressed means being taken seriously and all grown up,' said the local senior researcher who had informally taken me on as her protégée; and then, to heap some more society survival skills education on it, she added: 'And a demonstration of respect to Peruvians. Clothes matter.' Still a woman only, but at least a woman. It opened doors and I completed my internship with a fine project.

The other time I stumbled entirely unplanned into what was perceived as proper, decent dress code was at the University of Havana, Cuba. I was invited to teach a crash course on ontology engineering in 2010 (more about that later). I was wearing what I judged to be dressed-up nice clothes for the two weeks; Italian dresses, no less, reaching all the way to the knee. After the lectures in my spare time, I met informally with the lecturer, Rafael, who had invited me. For this I wore an older skirt of mine, faded from sunshine and detergent and, in my opinion, just about passable for holiday wear.

'Now this,' Rafael said, referring to the washed-out skirt, 'is a nice, proper skirt.'

This took me completely by surprise. 'But my other skirts are way fancier,' I said, 'and some of them are even new and shiny.'

'Yes,' he conceded, 'but they are not appropriate for a professor. The length of the skirt of a female professor has to be below the knee. This one is, the other ones aren't.'

I could not believe it. 'These are not the original colours anymore, even,' I pointed out.

'The skirt is older, I can see that, but proper is more important.'

'Hm.'

To be fair, it appeared that it wasn't only a woman's clothes that were subjected to guidelines; men had to wear pants, never shorts. 'Do you have any idea how uncomfortably hot it is in pants in summer?' Rafael winced.

'I do not. But the best I can do is feel sorry for all professors being subjected to clothing instructions.'

Since then, at every place I've worked I've tried to figure out the unwritten rules for clothing. There were none that I could actually discern, which doesn't mean one is out of the woods. I still anticipate it. Every morning I do a quick internal check: do I have to teach today? If yes, dress up a little bit more; if not, dress 'smart casual' for computer science standards (the bar is low). The upside is that my student evaluations hardly ever contain complaints about my clothes, unlike many of my female peers in STEM, who complain about this.[18] The one anecdote that I can add, in that I've not been 100% free of clothing comments, made me

---

[18]This latter claim seems to be largely anecdotal with very many anecdotes and a few articles in online news, rather than, say, getting one's hands on all evaluations to mine them for such comments on dress and test whether they are more prevalent in evaluations of courses taught by women. It has been investigated largely for the attire of lecturers in general, for attributes such as perception of knowledgeability of the subject domain, authority, friendliness, believability, and flexibility, with a sweet spot between not too informal and not too formal for the setting as best. For a recent review and evaluation, see: Mohammad Abul Kashem. The Effect of Teachers' Dress on Students' Attitude and Students' Learning: Higher Education View. Education Research International. Volume 2019, Article ID 9010589. (open access at https://www.hindawi.com/journals/edri/2019/9010589/). For a similar question and assessment at a South African university specifically: Anke Slabbert. Lecturer dress code and student perceptions of lecturer professional attributes. Journal of Psychology in Africa. 2019, 29: 176–181.

laugh rather than being annoyed. An undergraduate student complained that a few times I had worn clothes that were too tight in their view, because they could see clearly that I had breasts and that was distracting. Sigh. Adolescents.

On the whole, bad soap and a terrible water shortage apparently can lead to something positive. What would be better, though, is that those students would not be so judgemental about the clothes we wear.

....

This digression into fashion curiously does relate to the title of this chapter. We're still at the CIP, where being suitably dressed is important at least for women and there was no good excuse not to do so. If you had to do lab work, the proper clothes were protected with a lab coat, so that was no excuse for not dressing nicely. Sports wasn't really a thing for women, but if you did participate, you'd temporarily wear sports clothes to parade around in; hence, no problem either. You're safe with desk work as well, be it the reading, data analysis and writing of research, managerial tasks, or secretarial work. There are a few tasks where your nails can break, a skirt is not proper for, or where you might break into sweat, such as ducking under a table to fix computer cables.

When the situation demanded, an oxygen tank had to be picked up from storage and brought to the lab. Because this was a recurring task with gas tanks, the centre had made wheelie carts available, which made the process easier. As the lab where I did my experiments needed a gas tank, I suggested I could do the ferrying, even with my nice clothes on.

'No. We have men for that,' was the response of a colleague, Rosa.

Huh? I gave it another try: 'But with that cart it will be easy enough to do rather than search for a willing male colleague and interrupt their work?' I said.

She replied with a bit more insistence, 'No, let the men do the heavy work.'

That for sure had me raising my eyebrows, but Rosa was unfazed. Assuming that I needed more convincing, she continued: 'Why should I work myself into a sweat and get my hands dirty? I have enough hassles already. Trust me, this is the way to do it.'

A few minutes later a male colleague was already bringing the gas tank, smiling. He looked in our direction, and Rosa waved her hand thanking him, which he acknowledged. She nudged me to wave as well, which I did. Then she triumphantly heaped yet more on top of it, telling me in a satisfied voice: 'Look at him now, he's even gladly doing this for us. That's how we do things here. He's happy to show off his manly side and we don't have to get our hands dirty. It's a win-win situation.'

It did look like that. 'But what about self-reliance and demonstrating that?' I asked in a last attempt.

'Oh,' Rosa said, 'but I know I can do this. There's no need to show it off to boot.'

I was left wondering whether that's enough – if you don't try, you don't know if you can – but I gave up the tentative argument and let it slide then and there.

Similar situations were to return multiple times throughout my stay. For instance, I had a fine backpack for easy travel, but I was not supposed carry my backpack, or anything else for that matter, it seemed. That was what men were for as well. I was stubborn and carried my own backpack anyway, which elicited either of two typical responses. For one, never mind that my Spanish accent was one of the locals by this time, my clothes and the backpack gave away that I was a *gringa*. So there were always some head-shakes and mumbling – 'those foreign young women are all a bit crazy, whatever'. Alternatively, and more often later on during my stay when my clothing style had adjusted sufficiently, it seemed that some men felt insulted: not handing over the backpack to a man to carry it was interpreted as that I thought him a weakling who couldn't handle physically what I could. Handing over the backpack, then, was to be seen as an act of respecting his dignity and manliness.

There were other spheres where men had to be 'allowed to be men', such as paying for drinks in the bar. In the Netherlands, you pay for your drink(s). If you don't, then the guy who pays the bill is somehow entitled to more – after all, he paid for at least some of your drinks ... In Peru, at the time at least, I was informed in my initial weeks of arrival that they do things differently there.

'It would be an insult to pay for your drinks, because that would indicate that the man you're having a drink with is not man enough to be able to provide for you.' This was how Elena motivated the initial statement, as an 'induction training' of sorts while we were enjoying the view from the balcony of the house where we both rented a room.

'There's a good chance that even with my meagre scholarship, I might still have more disposable income,' I told her, 'so it may not be fair.'

'Oh, no worries,' was her response. 'If he did not have the money, he would not have asked you out.' I was not convinced. 'The first thing is to be seen together and to have a good time together, which means that he takes you out for the company. It will look good on him that he can take you out. If more were to follow, then that would be a bonus from his viewpoint, but it's most certainly not expected.'

'That's good to know. I'm afraid I might have missed a few potentially nice events then.'

'I'm telling you. Go out and have fun.'

That I felt guilty for not offering more after they paid was my problem, but it was something that I got used to fairly easily, enjoyed even. Yet would that enjoyment count as being on the fence on the issue – whether splitting the bill was better than chivalry of this sort? It did make me re-evaluate. The downside of this sort of chivalry is that it can be used as an argument that boys deserve more pocket money and male employees deserve higher wages because they purportedly have higher costs, paying for the food and drinks. In that light, I still prefer the split-bill. The principle of same-pay for same-work trumps the chivalry, no matter the fun evenings.

....

Letting men do the 'heavy work' turned out not to be an issue unique to Peru. I've seen it in South Africa as well, albeit less bluntly. The TL light at the start of this chapter is one such anecdote. I ended up painting my whole house myself and I fixed my own bicycle tyres. Indeed, in theory at least, I could have let someone else do it, especially now that I have enough money to pay for such activities. Painting ruins clothes and generates more sweat than pushing an oxygen tank. It also messes up one's haircut, in particular when you're not careful with alkyd-based paint or varnish. Old clothes I had and hair grows back. Moreover, logistically, it made sense to do it myself: I was moving over the summer holidays when painters aren't generally available, and moving in and painting later did not sound appealing. The bike? It was more time consuming, and risky, to go to a bicycle shop that was located on a very busy bicycle-unfriendly road than to fix it at home. Both were no different from other 'unladylike' projects I have attempted. In all of them, fixing a failure was still a possibility or there was no major loss. Trying is exciting and succeeding gives one a sense of accomplishment, of having done something concrete and tangible. Alternatively, the amusement to be got of the attempt outweighs both the fear of failure and the mutterings of a man.

9

SWITCHING SUBJECTS

The Stage: 1998 – The Netherlands;
2001 – Ireland; 2004 – Italy

From bites to bytes or, more precisely, from foods to formalisations, sprinkled with a handful of humanities and a dash of design. It does add up.

If you've read this linearly, or have seen my CV on my website, you'll know I studied 'Food Science, free specialisation' at the Wageningen Agricultural University in the provincial town of Wageningen in the centre – fine, middle – of the Netherlands. The word 'agriculture' was dropped from the name in 1997 to try to appeal to the masses, but it was still the university to go to for all things more or less related to the whole vertical production column of agriculture. Somehow I made it into computer science, but it wasn't at Wageningen. The motivation came from there, though, thanks to that university being at the forefront of science, first in its field in the world, and scoring high in the overall Top 100 of the Times Higher Education list of university rankings, among others. This bragging may sound haughty, but such an ambience facilitates exposure to a wide range of topics and techniques within the education system and among fellow students. Plus, it undoubtedly was the best quality education I ever had, which deserves to be said – and I've been around enough to have ample comparison material.

And yet.

The description of the road to computer science has nothing to do with any 'gender blahblah whatever', nor with an idealistic drive to solve the world food problem by other means, nor that I would have become fed up with the broad theme of agriculture. So what was it? This is something I'm regularly asked and for various reasons. There are those who are curious or nosy, some deem it improbable and believe I must be making it up, while others resentfully or nosily speculate where I obtained the money from. Therefore, I have included that scenic walk in this collection of essays.

It is also conceivable to speculate that those hurdles with mathematics and PC use were the motivation to turn to computing, as a way of doggedly conquering challenges for the sake of it. Nay, *au contraire*.

The shift happened when I was working on my last, and major, master's thesis in the Molecular Ecology Section of the Department of Microbiology at Wageningen University. The thesis topic was about trying to clean up chemically contaminated soil by using bacteria that would eat the harmful compounds, rather than cleaning up the site by disrupting the ecosystem with excavations and chemical treatments of the soil. In this case, it was about 3-chlorobenzoate, which is an intermediate degradation product from, mainly, spilled paint that had been going on since the 1920s; said molecule substantially reduces growth and yield of maize, which is undesirable. I set out to examine a bunch of configurations of different amounts of 3-chlorobenzoate in the soil together with the *Pseudomonas B13* bacteria and distance to the roots of the maize plants and their effects on the growth of the maize plants. The bacteria were expected to clean up more of the 3-chlorobenzoate in the area near the roots, called the rhizosphere, and there were some questions about what the bacteria would do once the 3-chlorobenzoate ran out. Mainly: would they die or feed on other molecules?

The bird's eye view sounded exciting to me, but there was *a lot* of boring work to do to find the answer. There were days when the only excitement was opening the stove to see whether my beasts had grown on the agar plate in the Petri dish; if they had (yay), I was punished with counting the colonies. This meant staring at dots on the agar plate in the Petri dish. That the mutant strain of the *Pseudomonas* turned blue on the substrate to make detecting and counting easier compared to the wild-type strain (white dot, as most others are) did not turn it into a joyful exercise. Then there were the analysis methods to be used, of which two turned out to be crucial for changing track, mixed with a minor logistical issue to top it off.

First, there was the PCR technique to sequence genetic material, which may be a familiar term by now during COVID-19 times. Machines do the procedure automatically now like a robot lab assistant. In 1997, it was still a special and a cumbersome procedure, which took about a day of near non-stop work by a human in order to sequence the short ribosomal RNA (16S rRNA) strand that was extracted from the collected bacteria. That was how we could figure out whether any of those white dots were, say, the *Pseudomonas B13* I had inoculated the soil with, or some other soil bacteria. Essentially, you extract the genetic material, multiply it, sequence it and then compare it to the sequences of which the species names were known. It was the last step that was the coolest.

The average number of base pairs of the 16S rRNA of a bacterium is around 1 500 base pairs which is represented as a sequence of some 1 500 capital letters consisting of A's, C's, G's, and U's. For comparison: the SARS-CoV-2 genome is about 30 000 base pairs. You really do not want to compare such long sequences of letters by hand against another, let alone manually check your newly PCR-ed sequence against many others to figure out which bacteria you likely had isolated or which one was phylogenetically most closely related. Instead, we sent the sequence, as a string of flat text with those ACGU letters, to a database called the rRNABase and we received an answer with a list of more or less likely matches within a few hours to a day, depending on the time of submitting it to the database.

It was like magic.

But how did it really do that? *What* is a database? *How* does it calculate the alignments? And since it can do this cool stuff that's not doable by humans, what else can you do with such techniques?

I wanted to know.

I needed to know.

The other technique I had to work with was not new to me, but I had to scale it up: the High-Performance Liquid Chromatography (HPLC). You give the machine a solution and it separates out the component molecules contained in the liquid sample, so you can figure out what's in the solution and how much of it is in there. Different types of molecules stick to the wall of the tube inside the machine at different places. The machine then spits out the result as a graph, where different peaks scattered across the x axis indicate different substances in the solution and the size of the peak indicates the concentration of that molecule in the sample.

I had taken multiple soil samples closer and farther away from the rhizosphere of different boxes with maize plants with different treatments of the soil, rinsed it and tested the solution in the HPLC. The task then was to compare the resulting graphs to see if there was a difference in treatment. When printed out, they covered a large table of about 1.5 x 2 metres, and I had to look closely at them and try to do some manual pattern matching on the shape and size of the graphs and sub-graphs. There was no program that could compare graphs automatically. I tried to overlay printouts and hold them in front of the ceiling light. With every printed graph about the size of 20 x 20 cm, you can calculate how many I had and how many 1-by-1 comparisons that amounted to. It felt primitive, especially considering all the fancy toys in the lab. Could those software developers not develop a tool to compare graphs as well?! Now that would have been useful. But no.

If only I could develop such a useful tool myself; then I would not have to wait on the software developers until they cared to develop what was needed.

On top of that manual analysis, it seemed unfair that I had to copy the data from the HPLC machine in the basement of the building onto a 3.5-inch floppy disk and walk upstairs to the third floor to the shared MSc thesis students' desktop PCs to be able to process it, whereas the PCR data was accessible from my desktop PC even though the PCR machine was on the ground floor. The PC could access the internet and present data from all over the world, so surely it should be able to connect to the HPLC downstairs?! Enter questions about computer networks. If

I could, I'd fix it.

The first step in trying to get some answers was to enquire with the academics in the department. 'Maybe there's something like "theoretical microbiology", or whatever it's called,' I asked my supervisor and more generally in the lab, 'that focuses on data analysis and modelling of microbiology? It's the fun part of the research and avoids lab work.'

'Not really,' was the consensus answer, with some acknowledging, 'Okay, sure, there is some. But theory-only without the evidence from experiments isn't *it*.'

Despite all the advanced equipment, of which computing is an indispensable component, they still deemed that wetlab research trumped solely theory and computing. Those technologies are there to assist answering the new and more advanced questions faster, but not to replace the processes, I was told.

Sigh. Pity. So be it. But I still wanted answers to those computing questions. I also wanted to do a PhD in microbiology and then probably move to some other discipline, since I sensed that possibly after another four to six years I might become bored with microbiology. Then there was the logistical issue that I still could not walk well since my ankle injury, which made wetlab work difficult; hence, it would make obtaining a PhD scholarship harder. Further, lab work was a hard requirement for a PhD in microbiology and it wasn't exactly the most exciting part of studying bacteria. I might as well swap to something else straight away then. Since there were those questions in computing that I wanted answers to ... the inevitable conclusion was: move to greener, or at least as green, pastures.

....

With the decision made, the next question was how to go about obtaining those answers. Would it not be nice if I could sign up for a sort of top-up degree for the computing aspects, to do that brand-new thing called 'bioinformatics'? There were no such top-up degrees in the Netherlands at the time. The only one that came close was a full degree in medical informatics, which was not what I wanted. I didn't want to know about all the horrible disease I could get.

The only way to combine it was to enrol in the first year of a degree in computing. The snag was the money. I was finishing up my five years of state funding for the master's degree (old system, so it included the BSc) and the state paid for only one such degree. The only way to be able to do it was to start working, save money and pay for the degree myself at some point in the near future once I had enough money. Going into IT in industry out in the big wide world sounded somewhat interesting as a second-choice option, since it should be easier with such skills to work anywhere in the world, and the experiences of the practice in Peru for six and a half months had made clear to me that I not only still wanted to travel the world, but would also be able to.

When I mentioned trying the IT industry to friends and acquaintances, my decision was met with a few raised eyebrows and laughter, as if I had just made a joke. Admittedly, they had witnessed episodes of me stubbornly giving uncooperative machines a stern talking-to. In those instances, however, I had been pushing the boundaries of the features available at the time. They were of a different category from attempting a few chaotic key combinations to start a petty print job or add page numbers, such as, for instance, incorporating molecule and pathway diagrams into the text processor. Rather than manually draw them, I had used ChemDraw, whose advertised new feature meant I would not have to do the primitive activity anymore of measuring the diagram's height, hitting Enter enough times to create the exactly right amount of whitespace, printing the page, gluing in the printed diagram, and making a copy so that it would look like the diagram was a proper part of the thesis. Or getting the feature of proper booklet printing to work as intended in the text processor, which ought to compute that, rather than manually creating the layout with landscape pages in two-column format. (Text processors have advanced quite well in the meantime.)

Once I finished the thesis in molecular ecology and graduated with a master's degree in January 1998, I started looking for work while receiving unemployment benefit. IT companies only offered conversion courses, such as a crash course in the Cobol programming language – the Y2K bug was alive and well – or some IT admin course, including Novell Netware, Unix or a Microsoft Certified System Engineer program (MCSE), the catch being that you'd have to keep working for the IT company for three years to pay off the debt of that training. That sounded like bonded labour to me and not particularly appealing.

One day flicking through the newspapers on the look-out for interesting job offers, a peculiar advertisement caught my eye: a conversion course over a year for an MCSE consisting of five months full-time training and the rest of the year a practice period in industry while maintaining one's unemployment benefit, and then all was paid off. A sizeable portion of funding came from Brussels, that is, the European Union. The programme was geared towards giving a second chance for basket cases, such as the long-term unemployed and the disabled. I was not a basket case, not yet at least. I applied for a position and was invited for an interview. My main task was to try to convince them that I was basket case-like enough to qualify to be accepted in the programme, but good enough to pass fast and with good marks. It roughly went as follows: I was sort of disabled with that sports injury of mine and therefore couldn't do the type of work I had studied for, since it required labwork that I couldn't do because of the injury, and I might just become a basket case soon, and women are a minority group in IT so that would be good for their statistics, and I already had a master's degree so likely would be a good student in the programme, which would look good in their statistics too.

I was accepted for the programme. A foot in the door.

We were a class of misfits of 16 people, 15 men and one woman – me. I completed the course successfully, and then completed a range of other vocational training courses while employed in various IT jobs. Unix system administration, ITIL service management, a pinch of Novell Netware and a smidgen of Cisco, a part of the Fibre Channel ANSI standards, and some more online self-study training sessions, which were all paid for by the companies I was employed at. The problem was that all the content to master for obtaining those certificates were, in my humble opinion, superficial and the how-to technology changes fast; and the prospect of perpetual rote learning did not appeal to me. I wanted to know the underlying principles so that I wouldn't have to keep updating myself with the latest trivial modification in an application. It was time to take the next step.

At the time I was working for Eurologic Systems in Dublin, Ireland, as a systems integration test engineer for fibre channel storage enclosures, which are boxes with many hard drives stacked up and connected for fast access to lots of data stored on the disks. They were a good employer, but they didn't offer much in the way of training opportunities since they were an R&D company and already employed experienced and highly educated engineers. I asked HR if I could sign up elsewhere, with, say, the Open University, and whether they might consider paying for some of it.

'Yes,' the humane HR lady said, 'that's a good idea. And we'll pay for every course you pass while you're in our employment.'

Deal!

When I mentioned this to my colleagues, they suggested I sign up for the Open University UK, rather than the Irish one, as the former was claimed to be better organised, had economies of scale, and was most likely better. I was a bit hesitant, as it would mean doing tertiary education in a foreign language, but the Open University of the Netherlands seemed even further behind on the distance learning with educational technologies. So the OU UK it was.

I breezed through my first year, even though I had skipped their first-year courses and jumped straight into second-year courses. My second year went just as smoothly. The third year I paid myself. I had opted for voluntary redundancy from Eurologic, which I was allowed to take in the second round, because I was keen to get back on track with my original plan to go into bioinformatics. The dotcom bubble had burst and Eurologic could not escape some of its effects. While they didn't like to see me go, they knew I'd leave soon anyway and they were happy to see that the redundancy money would be put to good use to finish my Computing & IT degree. With that finished, I'd be able to *finally* do the bioinformatics that I'd been after since 1997, or so I thought.

My honours project was on database development, with a focus on conceptual data modelling languages. I rediscovered the Object-Role Modelling language from the lecture notes of the Enschede University of Applied Sciences that I had bought out of curiosity when I did the MCSE in Enschede. The database was about bacteriocins, which are produced by bacteria that can be used in food for food safety and preservation. A first real step into bioinformatics. Bacteriocins have something to do with genes, too, and in searching for conceptual models about genes, in 2003 I stumbled into a new world, one with the Gene Ontology and the notion of ontologies to solve the data integration problem.

Marking and marks processing took a while longer than usual that year because the Open University UK's academics were on strike. After it had been resolved, I was finally awarded the BSc (Honours) degree (1st class) in March 2004. By that time, there were several bioinformatics conversion courses available. Ah well.

The long route I'd taken to get to this place did give me some precious insight that no bioinformatics conversion top-up degree can give: a deeper understanding of indoctrination into disciplinary thinking and ways of doing science. That is, on what the respective mores are, how to question, how to identify a problem, ways of looking at things, of answering questions and of solving problems. Of course, when there's, say, an experimental method, the principles of the methods are the same – hypothesis, set up experiment, do experiment, check results against hypothesis – as are some of the results processing tools (for example, statistics), but there are substantive differences. For instance, in computing, you break down the problem, isolate it, and solve that piece of something that's all human-made. In microbiology, it's about trying to figure out how nature works, with all its interconnected parts that may interfere and complicate the picture. In the engineering side of food science, it's more about once we figure out what it does and what we actually need, can we find something that does what we need or can we me make it do it to solve the problem? And if so, can we produce it at scale and safely? It doesn't necessarily mean one is less cool; just different. And hard to explain to someone who has ever studied only one degree in one discipline, most of whom invariably have the 'my way or the highway' attitude or think everyone is homologous to them. If you manage to create the chance to do a second full degree, take it.

....

Who am I to say that a top-up degree is unlike the double indoctrination into a discipline's mores? Because I *did* a top-up degree along with it, in yet another discipline. Besides studying for the last year in Computing & IT with a full-time load, I had also signed up for a conversion MA in Peace and Development Studies at the University of Limerick, Ireland. The Computing & IT degree didn't seem like it would be a lot of work, so I was looking for something to do on the side. I had started exploring what to do after completing the degree, and was thinking about whether to sign up for a master's or PhD in bioinformatics.

And so it was that I stumbled upon the information about the MA in Peace and Development Studies. Reading up on the aims and the courses, this coursework and dissertation master's looked like it might actually help me answer some questions that had been nagging me since I was in Peru. Before going to Peru, I was a committed pacifist; violence doesn't solve problems. Then Peru's *Movimiento Revolucionario Túpac Amaru* (MRTA) hijacked the Japanese embassy in Lima in late 1996 when I was in Lima. They were trying to draw attention to the plight of the people in the Andes and demanded more resources and investment there. I'd seen the situation there, with its malnutrition, limited potable water, and limited to no electricity, which was in stark contrast to the coastal region. The Peruvians I spoke to did not condone the MRTA's methods, but they had a valid point, or so went the consensus. Can violence ever be justified? Maybe violence could be justified if all else had failed in trying to address injustices? If it is used, will it lead to something good, or was it merely a set-up for the next cycle of violence and oppression?

Obviously, I did not have a Bachelor of Arts, but I had done some courses roughly in that area in my degree in Wageningen, such as agricultural politics of the EU and philosophy of science; I had also done a range of extra-curricular activities, including membership of the political party of progressive students and so on and so forth. Perhaps that, and more, would help persuade the selection committee? I put it all in detail in the application form in the hope that it would increase my chances and look like I could pull this off and be accepted into the programme.

I was accepted into the programme. Yay.

Afterwards, I heard from one of the professors that

it had been an easy decision, 'since you already have a master's degree, of science, no less'. Who cares about the rest? Or, to put it differently: this was another door that was opened thanks to that first degree I had obtained, which was paid for by the state merely because I qualified for the tertiary education. The money to pay Limerick University for this study came from my savings and the severance package from Eurologic. I had earned too much money in industry to qualify for state subsidy in Ireland – fair enough.

Doing the courses, I could feel I was missing the foundations, both regarding the content of some established theories here and there and in tackling things. By that time, I was immersed in computing, where you break down things in smaller sub-components; that systematising creeps and seeps into the reports you write. My essays and reports had sections and sub-sections and suitably itemised lists – *Ordnung muss sein*.

But no, now we're in a fluffy humanities space and it should have been 'verbal diarrhoea'. That was my interpretation of the feedback I received on one of my essays in particular: too much structure. An essay should rather be one long piece of text without a visually identifiable beginning, middle and end. This happened early in the first semester. A few months into the programme, I estimated that the only way I'd be able to pull off the dissertation was if I dragged the topic as much as I could into an area that I was comparatively good at: modelling and maths. In other words: stick with my disciplinary indoctrinations as much as possible, rather than fully descend into what to me still resembled mud and quicksand. For sure, there's much more to the humanities than meets an average scientist's eye, and I gained an appreciation of it during that degree, but that does not mean I was comfortable with the fuzzy qualitative approach and sense of lacking a foundational pillar here or there to gamble on a dissertation about that. In addition, for thesis topic choice, there were still the 'terrorists' I was looking for an answer to. Combine the two, and *voilà*, my dissertation topic: applying game theory to peace negotiations in the so-called 'terrorist theatre'. Prof Moxon-Browne was not only a willing, but an eager supervisor, and a great one at that. The fact that he could not wait to see my progress was a good stimulator to work and achieve that progress.

In the end, the dissertation had some 'fluffy' theory, some mathematical modelling, and some experimentation. It looked into three-party negotiations cf. the common zero-sum approach in the literature: the government and two aggrieved groups, of which one was the politically oriented one and the other one violent. For instance, in the case of South Africa, the apartheid government on the one side and the ANC and MK on the other side, and in case of Ireland, the UK/Northern Ireland government, Sinn Fein and the IRA. The strategic benefits of who teams up with whom during negotiations, if at all, depends on their relative strength: mathematically, in several identified power-dynamic circumstances, an aggrieved participant could obtain a larger slice of the pie for the victims if they were not in a coalition than if they were, and the desire, or not, for a coalition among aggrieved groups depended on their relative power. This deviated from the widespread assumption at the time that said that the aggrieved groups should always band together. I hoped it would still be enough for a pass.

More than enough, it seemed. It was awarded a distinction.

It turned out that my approach was fairly novel. Perhaps therein lies a retort argument for the top-up degrees against the 'do both' advice I mentioned before: a fresh look on the matter, if not interdisciplinarity or transdisciplinarity. I can see it likewise with the dissertation topics of our conversion master's in IT students. They have an honours degree in some other discipline and do a top-up in IT. The finance specialist who still works in finance takes a finance topic with some IT solution that supports the finance, written in a relatively structured and compartmentalised way. The former pharmacist connects all sorts of things because of the interconnectedness of it all, yet still has structured writing. The philosopher chooses as much ethics as he can get away with in the realm of IT and writes a lot. They're all interesting and topics that perhaps no disciplinarian would have produced. In like manner, they didn't think like a computer scientist or information technologist, not initially at least, in the same way as I didn't think like a humanities scholar.

....

The final step, then. With a distinction in the MA in Peace and Development in my pocket and a first in the BSc (Honours) in Computer Science & IT at around the same time, what next? The humanities topics were too depressing, even with a detached scientific mind – too many devastating problems and too little agency to influence – and I had worked towards bioinformatics for so many years already. Looking for jobs in bioinformatics, I discovered that they all demanded a PhD. With the knowledge and experience I had amassed during studying for the two full degrees I had completed, I could do all those tasks listed in the job ads that they wanted the bioinformatician to do. However, without that annoying PhD requirement, there was no chance I'd make it through the first selection round. That's what I thought at the time. I tried anyway and applied for a few posts, and was rejected for that reason. Maybe I should have tried and applied more widely. In hindsight, this was the system's way of saying they wanted someone well versed in both fields, not someone trained to become an academic, since most of those jobs were software development jobs anyway.

Disappointed that I still couldn't be the bioinformatician I'd expected I'd be able to be after those two degrees, I sighed and resigned myself to the idea that, gracious sakes, I'll get that PhD, too, then, and defer the dream a little longer.

In a roundabout way I ended up at the Free University of Bozen-Bolzano (FUB), Italy. They paid for the scholarship and there was generous project funding to pay for conference attendance. Meanwhile in the bioinformatics field, things had moved on from only databases for molecular biology to bio-ontologies to facilitate data integration with that aforementioned Gene Ontology as a major driver. The KRDB research centre at FUB was into ontologies, but then rather from the logic side of things. Fairly soon after my commencement with the PhD studies, my supervisor, Prof Enrico Franconi, who did not even have a PhD or a degree in computer science, told me in no uncertain terms that I was enrolled in a PhD in computer science programme, that my scientific contributions had to be in computer science, and if I wanted to do something in 'bio-whatever', that was fine, but I'd have to do that in my own time. Crystal clear.

Because I had only three years to complete the PhD, the 'bio-whatever' petered out and I had to step up the computer science content. On the bright side, passion will come the more you investigate something. Ontologies and conceptual modelling proper it was. I completed the PhD in the three year(-ish) timeframe; properly indoctrinated in the computer science way myself, I could now properly indoctrinate – um, guide – my own students, and I unashamedly do.

South Africa is slightly less disciplinarian than Italy, but only slightly. Academia is still mostly disciplinarian. Trying to navigate through an interdisciplinary thesis tends to have multiple stumbling blocks, from more work for the student to biased examiners who look down upon interdisciplinary publication venues. Some of those publication venues are indeed below par, which doesn't help the case. Overall, it's still unresolved even for bioinformatics, which is still trying to forge its niche 25 years on and is still more focused on novelties in bio rather than in informatics.

Dabbling in non-computing subjects is allowed and I think it's somewhat tolerated now. Among many combinations, there are natural language processing and computational linguistics, computational biology, and juridical informatics. I 'dabble' in the former, and yet again can sense the difference between double degree, top-up degree, and the dabbling. I did not do any formal course in linguistics. I largely learnt on the job: I've read a few textbooks and multiple relevant articles in linguistics and computational linguistics and I still speak a handful of languages. It's enough to get by and to some conference attendees at least to give the idea that I entered the area via linguistics or had at least some linguistics training since I clearly know what I am talking about. Or they just presume that women are the ones with the linguistics background. It's just that I can detect ways of thinking, and I don't think like my linguist collaborators – I want evidence, not intuition, and a rule that works, not a guideline for generally roughly probably sort of the case. On the bright side, they at least have some terminological ducks in a row, compared to the wild west of IT & dance that I make some of my students dabble in.

....

All this has skipped over one thing that I promised at the start of the chapter: the design. Weaving the interior design into the narrative didn't work well, and it was subsumed by the 'vocational training courses while employed in various IT jobs' phrase earlier on. Besides architecture, I also liked the idea of interior design as a possible career path when I was in secondary school, having been motivated initially by the arts classes in school. The tertiary degree for interior design follows 'higher general' secondary school, whereas I was doing the 'preparatory scientific' stream and supposed to go to university. The interest was parked but it lingered. It bubbled up to the fore in 1999 when I was reading the newspaper one day in Dublin while I was employed at Compaq at the German language Enterprise Support team. I spotted an ad for an evening course for an associate diploma in interior design that would certify for home interiors only. It seemed like a good entry step to explore and I thought it would be nice to socialise a bit more with Dubliners instead of only hanging out with the international crowd at Compaq. The costs? I scrambled that roundabout £1 200 together in a week: we received double pay for working a shift on New Year – the year 2000, no less – and double pay for 12-hour shifts instead of regular 8-hour shifts for a week. One week extra work for an interesting hobby for a year was a good deal in my opinion. It was a gear shift with all the colouring in with pencils and cutting and gluing, but it was enjoyable and good for a laugh, especially during the breaks. I passed with a distinction and, in conjunction with the associate diploma, got Rhodec certified. I still enjoy playing around with interiors as a hobby but have given up my initial idea from 1999 to use IT with it: tangible samples work fine.

What next? I don't know. I completed degrees in science, engineering and political science straddling into humanities, and I have an associate diploma in interior design, so I have sort of broadly touched on all the areas. Another degree switch would not be as fundamentally new as the first time around. I still have many questions, but I also realise that many will remain unanswered, even if the answer is known to humanity already, since to live means it's finite and there's simply not enough time to learn everything.

In any case, my takeaway is this: study what you want, not what anyone tells you to study. It's your life you're living, not someone else's.

10

A FUTURE WITH SCIENTISTS

The Stage: 2004 – Cuba

El futuro – the future – is now. It was so, too, in 2004 when I was still very much at the 'budding scientist' stage, educating myself out of the marriage market, and travelling around the world whenever I could. Science and travelling can go well together, especially *after* the science obligation rather than before. Not that I would have taken that advice if it were to have been given to me at the time – some things are better learned by doing.

In late 2003 my savings and that severance package from Eurologic Systems that I had been living off and studying from had dwindled substantially. I had managed to secure a steady income, albeit a meagre one (the postgraduate scholarship in computer science was about a third of my last-earned salary). I did not want to let that remainder of the savings fizzle out on shopping, drinks, and other trivialities; instead, I wanted to put it to some special use. It boiled down to two options: a fancy laptop that would last for a while or a four-week shoestring budget trip to Cuba.

The choice was easy: the laptop could wait.

Who knew how long Fidel would be around and I was sure it would be an interesting experience to see for myself what Cuba's socialism was like rather than buying into conflicting stories in the news, compare it to my experiences in Bulgaria in 1987 when the Iron Curtain was still in place, and ponder some more about that never-ending conversation on whether the Cuban revolution was the way to go or whether South Africa's style of transition to democracy was a better way to address injustices.

In exploring options and otherwise preparing for the trip, I came across an announcement about the Interjoven '04 conference – a scientific conference with a track on agri-informatics, which is actually equally as good to aim for as bioinformatics. It sounded like the perfect excuse to go to Cuba and mix it with the pleasure of a holiday. I submitted a short paper that emanated from my Computer Science & IT honours project and which I had extended a little. My supervisor at the time was miffed about my initiative, not only for having sent off something on my own (even though I had done the research and written the paper on my own) but also to what she perceived as a dubious venue because it was an unknown conference and the level of science in Cuba was unclear to her. A scientific conference is a scientific conference, I surmised, and computer scientists go to scientific conferences. As a postgraduate student, I was a computer scientist in the making, and to a conference I would go.

The short paper was accepted and I had the opportunity to explore and learn about the country both as a tourist and as a budding scientist. Considering other commitments, it worked out best to have about two weeks of holiday, then the conference, and then a week or so after that. The conference had associated accommodation in a small village called San José de las Lajas, which was situated about 40 km south-east of Havana, which I had booked for the conference duration. The rest I'd figure out once I got there. My Routard travel guide, a present from my flatmate, would turn out to be a valuable and lasting gift. In my youthful enthusiasm, I expected to be able to recall enough Spanish to find my way around and not walk into some disaster that would mess up my first ever participation in a scientific conference.

Being on a tight budget, I opted for a *casa particular* outside Havana city centre. This is a house or apartment where a family lives and rents out a room or two to tourists. It is more affordable than a hotel and the tourist information said it was more interesting too. The one I went to and knocked on the door unannounced of was near the main intercity bus station, the Plaza de la Revolución and the Rambla shopping street. They were open for business and they had space. It was a basic yet comfortable room and the family was polite and friendly.

During the day, I did my touristy things on my shoestring budget and my Spanish turned out to be sufficient. My Spanish also still had a Lima accent, so I could operate below the radar of the 'this is a European or North American and so must have lots of money' and can be fleeced, as tourists typically are identified all around the world. But then, the system was almost asking for aiming to operate below that radar. The prices at one food stall I went to were listed ambiguously, in $. At another place, near Vedado, the prices seemed way too expensive to me, especially having to pay in the hard currency of *pesos convertibiles* rather than in the local *pesos cubanos*. The conversion rate was about 1:24. I had noticed the locals were buying there a lot, so, with a straight face, I ordered food and gave the amount in *pesos cubanos*, just to see what would happen.

It was accepted!

These are moments it makes it totally worth it to have learned a language, literally, in the economic sense. I sat down on the curbside and got into conversation with one of the other patrons. All went smoothly, until it didn't. They assumed I was an exchange student from one of the central south Latin American countries until I got stuck and couldn't find the word I wanted to say and couldn't find a way to talk my way around that word either. I confessed and the stall owner gasped an 'ahhh, no!' for the extra money they could have made if only they'd caught me when I'd ordered, before I paid for the food. I explained that I was still a poor student who was gluing on a holiday I barely could afford to attend a scientific conference in two weeks. That made it less bad of a missed opportunity. That I could speak the language and moved about humbly, conforming to everyone else, also counted in my favour. In the end, all was well, and we parted as friends.

My next stop was the 'Mecca' of the revolutionaries, Santa Clara, about 6-8 hours' drive from Havana. This is the place where the train was derailed and robbed and which ended up being a turning point in the revolution's history. There was not much to do in this small provincial town, but the conversations were friendly and interesting and more frequent. Also here, there was no real poverty. People went about doing their work, children went to school and so on.

The only queue there was, was for the cybercafé to go on the internet. I queued with the Cubans, for over two hours, and I entered through the same process as everyone else onto the Web and it worked. Somehow I felt the need to send an email from Cuba just to show that, yes, they had internet and it was accessible; 1:0 for Cuba and against the news articles that would be published afterwards saying that internet wasn't available.

So far, so good. Then I went further afield from Havana, onward to Trinidad, which was when and where things started to change.

....

By then I'd had a week and a half or so of doing touristy things on my tiny budget, connecting with Cubans, and relaxing. It was great and there was a remarkably different, upbeat vibe compared to the communism that reigned over Eastern Europe until the early 1990s. The first wrinkle was a question from the owner of the *casa particular* I was staying at in Trinidad. I was sitting on one of those cast-iron chairs on the patio when the woman who managed the *casa* walked over to me and told me in a slightly nervous and cautious tone that they had had a visit from the Ministry of the Interior enquiring about me.

Huh?

I shared my itinerary with her, where I had been and where I was planning to go, and she released a small sigh of relief. 'Indeed, it all seems to be an honest misunderstanding!' she said. At my quizzical look, she went on to explain. 'You were supposed to have gone straight to the address of the accommodation that you had given on your visa'. That was the conference accommodation. I had taken the address instruction literally, however: the visa required only *a* booking, not for the whole length of my stay and not necessarily the first place I stayed. 'Perhaps,' she said, when I pointed this out, 'but the understanding is that it is the *first* place of stay. The Ministry had noticed that you had not turned up at that address upon arrival. They had lost track of you.'

'What?!'

'Yes, and you had resurfaced in the system with the booking of the omnibus to Santa Clara, since you provided your passport details there. So they asked around there, and they found the *casa particular* where you had stayed. There were only a few foreigners because it's still the low season, so you were relatively easy to find. The owner gave them our address in Trinidad, which she'd suggested to you ... hence their visit to us.'

'Ah, ehm.'

There were still the first days to be accounted for and I gave them the contact information of the first *casa particular* in Havana I'd stayed at. Later that day, I was informed that that had indeed been legit so all was sorted and no need to worry (anymore).

The second wrinkle was practically a bigger issue. Shortly after arriving in Trinidad, it was time to obtain cash again. Before I'd left for Cuba, I had asked the MBNA Europe whether their credit card worked in Cuba, since there was the blockade and all; twice I was assured that it would. It did not. I did have some British pounds, but I'd received those in Edinburgh. The Scots insist on having a different face on their paper money from that of the rest of the UK. It turned out that Trinidad did not accept these.

In other words, stranded and with no money left, I had to return to Havana to go to the embassy to figure out something. As luck would have it, the day before I was due to leave I had met a Dutch couple and had played tourist guide for them, showing them some good places I had already found or knew of and introducing them to some tasty food. They were heading for Piñar del Rio, which was in the same direction as Havana, and they were willing to give me a lift for free and drop me off at a *casa particular*. Step one accomplished. Perhaps it would not be the end of the trip before I'd even make it to my first ever scientific conference after all.

The next day I walked to the 'embassy area' of Havana, which was quite a distance. The first embassy from the European Union that I came across was the UK's. Since they would know that my Scottish-English paper money was valid, it made sense to try there to at least have it changed for the paper money with the Queen on it, and to resolve the card issue – we're all EU, after all, at least in those days we were.

Nope. They sent me away because I did not have a British passport. In fact this was in contravention of EU agreements, which state that any consulate or embassy of a country of the EU shall assist an EU citizen who's in trouble. I struggled onward with very tired legs that hurt – even my hands hurt from the crutches – heading to the Dutch consulate. It happened to be Second Pentecost Day and so the consulate was closed. After a short conversation with the security guard (hooray again for being able to speak Spanish sufficiently!), mentioning my money issues and lack of food and such, a consular officer was called. He was not happy to have to come in on his day off, but he did. I explained the situation and that I had tried the UK embassy's office and that they had sent me away. It annoyed him more that they were in contravention of the EU agreement, making it even worse to have it happen on his day off.

It was not a public holiday in Cuba, so we tried a few ATMs and we tried the Scottish-British money with a few banks, including the head office, but no luck. The head office of the main bank did have more experience with financially stranded visitors, however: MBNA Europe bank is indeed registered in Europe, but in their back office they slush the money to their USA-based parent company. That extra money that I had transferred into that account for emergencies had therefore been wired to the US-based parent. When an ATM request comes in from anywhere in the world, the request is ultimately routed to the USA, which falls under the blockade. The result: no access. No matter that it was my money that the bank only had on loan from me. The eventuality I had not counted on, was an, at best, clueless MBNA Europe bank employee, and shady money wiring wheeling and dealing of a financially highly networked world. Furthermore, the bank knew of the Scottish-British pounds paper money missing the Queen's picture, but they would not accept it because it was not accepted internationally.

The only way to resolve this was to compel someone to wire money from outside Cuba, someone who did not have their account affiliated with the USA either directly or indirectly. Back in the consulate, I gave the consular officer my brother's landline and mobile numbers, but there was no response to either call. (It turned out that he had gone away with the family for the weekend and had left his mobile phone at home.) The consulate's employee did not look pleased. Was there perhaps anyone else I could contact? Someone I was fairly sure would be contactable on a public holiday was a friend from the 'nerd brigade' – people in IT, already in those days, were practically hooked into the internet at all times. I did not have his phone number at hand, so we had to look it up online from his website, whose domain name had the non-confidence-inspiring name of *duffe aap*, which translates roughly to 'silly monkey'. He picked up on the second ring and a surreal conversation ensued with lots of laughs. A shortened version of it went as follows.

Him: Hello, Stephan here.

Me: Hi, it's Marijke.

Him: Oh hi, how are you doing?

Me: Ehm, I'm calling from Cuba (giggling). Calling from the Dutch consulate, to be more precise.

Him: Whoah, cool. How is it there? What?

Me: Interesting. And I managed to run out of money and my credit card doesn't work because of the blockade of the Americans.

Him: (laughs hard)

Me: I tried to call my brother, but he doesn't grasp the point of a mobile phone, that it's supposed to be mobile.

Him: (insider laughs of the connected about the average Joe Soap of those days)

By now, the consulate official is smiling, showing the first faint trace of amusement, realising from the conversation that things are going to turn out all right.

Me: Yeah. So I figured you would be connected.

Him: Of course!

Me: Now my awkward question is if you can help me with the money issue. To transfer x euros to the Dutch consulate in Cuba, then they'll draw it from the bank and give it to me, and when I return from Cuba, I'll pay it back immediately.

Him: Sure, no problem (with a smile in his voice and a

laugh about the situation)

Me: Thank you!!

And so it proceeded. I handed the conversation over to the consulate official, who gave Stephan the bank details, and we said goodbye. The official lent me some money so that I'd be able to eat and pay the *casa particular* for the day, and the next day the money issues were sorted. Upon my return to the *casa* – the same one from the beginning of my stay, who had also had a visit from the Ministry of the Interior – they were shocked to hear what had happened, and straight away made me a late breakfast sort of meal in the middle of the afternoon. The next day I received Stephan's money from the consular employee, and paid the *casa* for the extra day.

The time had come to travel onward to finally participate in my first ever scientific conference.

Mental note: gluing-on vacation days to a conference afterwards is no doubt a better idea than doing it beforehand.

....

That last stretch of the trip to the conference venue was relatively luxurious. I travelled in a taxi to the Institute for Agricultural Sciences (ICA), which was located about 40 km outside of Havana in San Jose de las Lajas. It felt a bit like in the 'middle of nowhere' since transportation was limited; the institute wasn't even in the village itself, and for that reason there were a few flats with apartments for employees. One of the flats had a mural with the face of a young Fidel on it and one of his pronouncements – made in 1961 according to the mural:

El futuro de nuestra patria tiene que ser necessariamente un futuro de hombres de ciencia.

'The future of our home country necessarily has to be a future of scientists'.[19]

Hah, yes! Someone had his priorities right.

The conference? Honestly, I cannot recall much of the agri-informatics. The other bio/agri-informatics papers and poster presentations were exploring the area – IT for agriculture was still fairly novel in those days – and they were all applied from the perspective of computer science research, as is common in that field of specialisation both then and now. While overall none of the papers at the conference may have affected my actual PhD topic, there was the usual buzz of science with nerds with the same interests meeting up among the like-minded and the networking effect. Six years after graduating from Wageningen University, I was combining IT and agriculture/biology scientifically and making some progress with my plans. There was a general respect for education and science and it didn't matter who was doing it. To me, that was a refreshing attitude, and it is part of the tally of the gains of the revolution.

I do remember a PhD thesis defence that was held around the time of the conference at the ICA. It was impressive for the way it went and the topic of the thesis. The otherwise waste product of, if I remember correctly, cocoa bean shells was used in chicken farms as ground coverage. It turned out that it made the chickens healthier: walking on it took more effort, which was good for muscle-building; it also appeared to be edible mass to chickens

---

[19]In 1960 according to the Granma newspaper: http://www.granma.cu/ granmad/secciones/fidel_en_1959/fidel_en_1960/art-001.html (last accessed on 8 May 2021).

and they seemed to be picking up bits of it and somehow the whole thing resulted in lower incidence of *salmonella* infections in the animals. What had started as a question of 'can we put plant waste material x to good use?' ended with the answer 'yes, and it's healthier too'. The reduced *salmonella* infections were especially of interest to me, as I recalled lectures from my food microbiology courses. We had to learn about and figure out how to mitigate *salmonella* infections from the perspective of food safety, like keeping chicken meat separately and monitoring tiramisu production processes because of its raw eggs as ingredient. It turned out that a better living environment helped too and, who knows, possibly more than the food processing interventions. It made me miss it all. Then again, the poster session with the IT for agriculture was also interesting and I did not want to think about, let alone carry out, the practical experiments that PhD student had had to do to obtain those results.

The conference opening session was fun when we were near the end of all the speeches: for each unique country of origin of the participants came a '*Viva [country x]!*' proclamation by the functionary and '*Viva, Viva, Viva!*' replies by all the participants in the conference hall. Most participants were from Latin America, with a guy from Spain and me from Europe as overseas participants. Doing all those vivas and receiving them felt inclusive and energising.

The Spanish guy and I received special treatment from the local conference organisation, also because we both stayed a little longer than most conference attendees, thanks to the organiser responsible for the IT and agriculture part, Abiel Roche Lima. It was similar to how we went the extra mile at the Free University of Bozen-Bolzano when there were visitors to university, with a bit extra. Resulting from that combination of soft skills training on how to behave in academia, I try to emulate this whenever I have visitors.

All in all, an adventure it was. It felt good that I had been making progress towards my goals. I was to learn later that not all computer science conferences are alike. This one wasn't the sort of conference you would be going to score brownie points to advance your career in academia. Would I do it again? For sure. Moreover, one thing can lead to another, as I shall demonstrate in Chapter 12 (Baptism by fire).

This time was definitely not the only time I visited Cuba to enjoy the science vibe; it had set in motion a domino effect.

PART THREE

THE WILD WEST

11

ONE OF THE BOYS, SORT OF

The Stage: 2000 – Ireland, mostly

I have been 'out there', in industry, unlike the majority of academics. After my degree in food science and a conversion course to Microsoft Certified System Engineer, I had to go out into the big wide world to commence with gainful employment along with everybody else.

Many things are different; some not. I could easily have written a chapter along the lines of 'We value that we can get away with paying you less': I am one of the anecdotes that make up the data that women employees, on average, earn only about 80% of what men earn in the same job. That 80% doesn't take into account that regularly we already do the work of that job next up on the ladder but aren't promoted, for whatever lame excuse. It's boring to read about, and there were many other 'interesting' experiences, of which my stint at Compaq stands out. Those happenings are of an era gone by, a generation ago almost, and at a time when there was another bug threatening society. It was late 1990s and the Y2K bug loomed large.

The first step was getting a job. The IT industry wants you to be smart, but not too smart. I had learned that the hard way with the IBM entry test and its haughty HR guy who ran the selection process. I did the test and afterwards in the interview meeting he asked me how I thought I'd done. I told him the results I was expecting, which turned out to be very close to what he had on the printout. That annoyed him tremendously, because he wanted to bring me that good news and now he couldn't and, apparently, I wasn't supposed to score too high on those tests because he wanted to feel smarter. Whatever, fine, I can do that.

I used some subterfuge on the entry test for Compaq, in that I tried to gamble to make sure I would do it just about good enough, but not too well, by intentionally skipping some questions. I would receive the outcome by snail mail. The test centre called me before the envelope arrived. My first thought was *Oh, sh**, now what?* After polite introductions, the conversation started for real.

'I'm calling you to inform you about the results, because we imagined you'd most likely be too shocked to read them in the letter,' the woman at the other end of the line commenced.

Huh?

'You're in the 96th percentile,' she said.

My first thought was *Oh no. That's still too high*, but I managed to utter just the 'Oh' and bite my tongue for the rest.

'Yes,' said the test person, 'very, very impressive', as if they hardly ever saw such results.

'Uhm, yeah, thank you for calling,' I managed to say, while starting to worry that I wouldn't get the job – 90th percentile would have been good, but any higher and they'd figure out I probably would not stay long.

'You're welcome,' she responded.

'And now what?' I asked. 'Will it affect my chances of being offered the job at Compaq?'

'The Compaq Ireland office decides. They'll let you know soon,' she said.

I was offered, and accepted, a job in the Enterprise

support team for German-speaking customers at their EMEA support centre in Clonskeagh, Donnybrook, Dublin, Ireland. Its seven-storey building housed around 700 employees. We were mostly in our 20s and since the centre provided support for Europe and North Africa, we came from all those countries. The workplace atmosphere was infused with a vibe of 'exciting summer camp for nerds who have gone on an adventure'. Good times.

The support centre was organised by language, rather than country, and there were separate groups for notebook, desktop, and enterprise support. Customers would call us for various support requests, ranging from simple replacement part ordering to not knowing how to configure tape back-up solutions to trying to isolate and fix some other IT problem that involved Compaq hardware or software. The customers who called our hotline were typically the system administrators from the IT department of a small, medium, or large sized company.

Compaq customers called a local phone number that was then routed through to Ireland, which most callers were not aware of. And they didn't know what a call centre was like either. Each floor was an open-plan office with low dividers between each desk that could be either lined up in rows or positioned in groups. Each desk had a phone with lots of buttons, a headset and a computer, and any other materials of your liking. One of the buttons on the phone was the mute button: we could still hear the customer but we could say whatever we liked without any repercussions. That could equally well be used for asking your neighbour a question about the problem at hand or a *Trottel!* exclamation if the customer had done something silly or was too clueless. We answered around 15-20 calls on most days. Most of them went fine. There were others, about once a week, where the conversation went along like this (in German):

Me: Good day. This is Compaq support and you are speaking with Ms Keet. How can I help you?

Male customer: Please put me through to the engineer.

Me: I am the engineer.

MC: No, a real engineer.

Me: You have been put through to a real engineer already, which is me.

MC: Ha ha. Just put me through! I have waited long enough in the queue already.

Me: Look, I really am a real engineer. You have two options: you can either explain your problem to me and have it resolved, or you can call again and wait in the queue again and hope that one of my male colleagues picks up, which is statistically very likely to happen. It's your choice.

Most of those types of caller would grumble but then proceed to explain their problem, as the alternative of another 5-20 minutes in the queue was even less appealing than speaking to a woman. Some hung up. Occasionally, after the 'I am the engineer', there came excitement, in that the sysadmin was happy to talk to a woman, as if that was the first time they'd done that in a while.

Another woman and me were the first women ever in the German Enterprise Support team. It was August 1999. I was told at a later time that they had discussed it beforehand in the team, and several members had worried that allowing women in the team would be too disruptive to the team spirit and cause trouble, but in the end they had decided to give it a try and see how the experiment went. Later I also found out that I was hired for the lowest salary in the about 15-person-strong team. There was only one employee on the whole Enterprise Support floor who earned less than me: a very blonde young woman in the English team, who was at barely two-thirds of the top-paid enterprise support engineer. They had lots of in-house training opportunities and I had received a nice relocation package and was housed in a posh apartment for a few weeks upon arrival, which made up at least a morsel in the balance against the low pay in general, although not nearly balancing out the difference. Apparently, I was expected to have negotiated better. I didn't even know I could negotiate.

....

Since I had obtained my certificate of Microsoft Certified Systems Engineer already – for the curious insider: NT4 with IP and Enterprise Server – and then had passed the Compaq induction courses on first try, the Compaq brownie points system computed that I was deserving of the much-coveted and revered Compaq ASE sweater. Few men had an ASE certificate – accredited systems engineer – and no one could recall anyone else who had obtained an ASE right after the induction training. Those sweaters only come in men's shapes and sizes and were supposed to be worn with jeans and to be paraded around on the Enterprise Support floor.

The day I picked up my sweater, coincidentally, I was wearing a short skirt (with stockings!). I put the sweater on anyway, regardless of the fact that it was also way too big and baggy for my figure, and I walked around wearing it whenever I needed to walk somewhere. Some of my colleagues in the German team, most of whom originated from Germany, Austria, and Switzerland, had big smiles and congratulated me on the achievement or on the guts to wear it with a short skirt, or both.

Then Franz, tall, blond and Swiss-German, walked over to me, looked down on me, and said with a serious expression on his face: 'The ASE sweater stands for something, and it is supposed to be worn with jeans, not a skirt. This,' pointing to my skirt, 'is not appropriate and diminishes its standing. We have something to uphold when wearing it and you're not contributing to that like this.'

'I have earned the sweater as much as anyone else who has one and I can wear it how I want,' I rebutted.

'Yes, I know that, but still, that sweater goes better with jeans...' he muttered.

And that was roughly the end of that conversation. A short while later, the other female colleague also obtained the ASE certificate, but she preferred not to wear the sweater to work, so as not to upset anyone.

....

Initiation done and dusted, I was part of the team. In those days, jokes were sent around via email, and before I arrived, the team members used to send them to the team's group email address. They continued to do so when I became a team member. A sizeable number of those jokes were sexist jokes, both general and IT-insider ones. The gentler ones, at least the ones I can still remember, went as follows:

Q: What's the difference between butter and the legs of a dumb blonde?

A: The legs are easier to spread.

Q: What's a blonde with a haystack under her arm?

A: Extended memory.

This went on for a while. Occasionally, I would receive emails from female friends with jokes that were just as dubious, but about men:

Q: Why did God create man before woman?

A: One always experiments with a draft before the masterpiece.

One day, I decided the time had come for a payback of sorts, and I hit Reply to one of those group emails with sexist jokes and copied in a bunch of similar jokes about men. In less than one minute after hitting Send, I could hear the first gasps. A few colleagues stood up, so they could see over the short dividers in the open-plan office. More Noise. I stretched to peek over the dividers and then stood up too, to check out the effects my response seemed to be having. The colleagues who had stood up had big shocked eyes, as they looked around at each other and at me; some of them covered their mouths with their hands. Then they looked at those still seated, who were stuck on a call they had to finish before they could find out what had just happened.

Finally it was dawning on them that I had been receiving all their sexist jokes all along and that – shock, horror! – there actually do exist such jokes about men too. Franz, of all colleagues, that same guy of the sweater, walked over to me and apologised profusely for what they had been doing all this time. He only realised that it was not quite right when the tables were turned, and realised that realising it only then was a bit tardy. The German colleague sitting next to me rolled his chair back to get out of the divider, as did I when he called my name. He turned to me and started laughing.

'Okay, so we're good, then?'

'Yeah, no worries,' I grinned.

....

It was time for a team dinner. I can't recall now whether it was the time we went to the Lebanese restaurant – democratically chosen because they had a belly dancer – or the Mongolian. Either way, the after-dinner session was planned to be in the style of how gentlemen have their after-dinner time, like with coffee and then whiskey and cigars. We had left the restaurant and moved to a bar with seating outside. Drinks were ordered and a box of cigars was put on the table, to be passed around. I was a bit hesitant when the box came to me, but only because I don't appreciate cigars. Turns out it was an offer I could not refuse.

'Men have whiskey and cigars,' one of my team members said, 'and you're part of the team with us men. You're like us.'

'Well, not a man,' two other team members chimed in at about the same time, 'but close enough for the team bonding purpose.'

That ended up as the shared opinion of the group.

If you want to survive in IT, you either blend into the team or leave. I chose to blend in and I smoked that cigar.

12

BAPTISM BY FIRE

The Stage: 2010 – Italy; South Africa;
Cuba somehow too

It's time to move to the other side. Academia. On paper, it's the dream job: tenured academic. The job spec is about 40% teaching the next generation of movers and shakers in their phase of becoming adults, 40% research into what piques your interest, and 20% administration, management, and outreach. In theory. In theory, there is no difference between theory and practice; in practice, there is.

Introduction into academia when you start as a full-time lecturer at my current employer, in our department at least, over at least the past 10 years that I know of, is along the lines of 'sweetie, to get used to it all, you'll have a 50% teaching load compared to the departmental average in the first year, which increases to 75% in the second year, and then 100% from then onward, and here's a course for you to teach for which teaching material exists that you can take over from your predecessor'.

Elsewhere, it can be a tad bit rough. Brutal, even.

My first brush with teaching was as a teaching assistant. The professor prepared the lectures and had the responsibility to teach them. My task was to run the tutorials, which included setting exercises, walking around and explaining the theory, and setting and marking the mid-term test. The tutorial was scheduled right after the two-hour lecture. I typically arrived some 10-15 minutes early and would wait outside in the hall until the lecture was finished. One day I walked into the hall at my usual early time, planning to sit and rest before entering the classroom, but the classroom door was already open. Odd. I peeked in and saw that the students were hanging around and chatting. They stopped when they saw me.

'Did the prof finish early today?' I asked.

'Nah, he didn't show up,' came the response.

That was awkward. My tutorial exercises were aligned to what they were supposed to have been taught in the preceding lecture.

'Will you teach us now?' an eager student asked.

Panic!

After a deep breath, I replied, 'No. I prepared for exercises. Where exactly did he stop last week? It probably still aligns sort of sufficiently with that and we can partially revise and finish up last week's content, if needed.'

It barely matched, but they'd largely forgotten last week's content anyway, so I ended up having to do some impromptu teaching as a taste of being thrown in front of the proverbial wolves. If you only ever sat in class: we don't 'just rock up and talk'. For first-time teaching of a course when there's material to rely on, it takes about 5-8 hours preparation for each lecture hour. You need to, at least, think of and practise ways to explain the material, figure out how to structure it, find or devise good examples, prepare content and tweak slides, and explore ideas for how to engage the class. Lab or tutorial preparation is a bit different. That day I managed to convert half of the lab time into a quasi-lecture.

They were kind students at least. That is, they did not try to taunt or destroy me. They wanted to learn, I had the knowledge, and I was there; it was that simple. For the next week, I added a few slides from the prof's lecture in the tutorial slides as a precaution. When I arrived, the remaining students were killing time playing a first-person shooter game on the big screen of the data projector, and some had studied elsewhere and were trickling in for the tutorial. Impromptu teaching it was again. After that, I prepared the tutorial time with the prof's slides as well, and vowed to always prepare not only the material but also for contingencies if I ever had to teach or tutor again.

....

Once I had my PhD, I was hired as an assistant professor (*ricercatore a tempo determinato*) at the Free University of Bozen-Bolzano (FUB) in Italy, which was a full-time job on a three-year contract. I was expected to do 'any teaching duty as assigned', which, practically speaking, meant teaching a postgraduate course. There was no 'sweetie ...' policy. The new and revised full semester course in Semantic Web technologies as part of the European Master's in Computational Logic was to be split into two parts: the first part should be about the logics with their standardised computational versions and the second part about developing ontologies, which are meaningful logical theories about some domain of interest, such as genes, anatomy, or organisations. Since I had some experience with the latter and wasn't teaching yet, I was assigned to develop that brand-new part. Not 'hindered' by, say, a text-book (non-existent) or lecture notes (non-existent) or even a syllabus as to what ontology engineering for computer scientists should look like (non-existent), I was thrown into the deep end to figure it out and make something of it that would be up to their standards.

That was my first real, official teaching experience as a lecturer of a course: I had *carte blanche* to fill 24 lecture hours, any additional assignments or labs, and an exam – whatever I deemed fit to do with it. The only constraints were the topic, ontology engineering, and that it had to fit within the overarching scope of the European Master's in Computational Logic programme. That was a lot of work. In trying to make it a balanced course rather than ending up with one of peddling my pet projects only, I had to read more broadly, digest and structure it, make many new slides, and think of how to actually explain it all. Furthermore, I experimented with one of those things that educational technologies people keep proposing as a wonderful idea: write a blog post for a lecture and then the students can engage and discuss the content in the comments section. It doesn't work. Each double lecture took, on average, at least three days of preparation besides the research I was supposed to be doing full time. That said, I did enjoy the challenge and learned a lot and, in hindsight, lots of good things came out of the successive iterations. The second instalment of teaching ontology engineering was, in fact, a turning point; and not because I managed to do it in Cuba, although that might have nudged it a little.

From that trip to Cuba in 2004, I had stayed in contact with Abiel, albeit only sporadically, as we were both rather busy trying to do a PhD. I had booked a holiday to Cuba to leave straight after my thesis defence in early April 2008, come what may, regardless of the verdict. We met up again, had a good time, and he mentioned that they were working toward organising the Informática 2009 conference. That was in the order of a good excuse to return. The track that had something to do with ontologies was in geomatics. Abiel asked if I could come up with something in that area. Sure I could. My paper was accepted and I returned to Cuba for the conference in 2009. At the conference, I met a lecturer and PhD student from the University of Havana, Rafael, who later convinced me to return in 2010 to teach the course on ontology engineering that I had tried to develop and teach at FUB. I was humbly honoured by the request, yet also a bit hesitant because I was well-aware of the fact that I was only an early-career academic.

'I'm fairly new at teaching and there certainly are other academics much better suited than me,' I replied initially.

'Yes, perhaps,' Rafael replied, 'but I prefer the Semantic Web angle of your syllabus, it's part of a European Master's programme so it means it does have quality, and anyhow you know more on the topic than we do, so we'll always learn at least something from it.'

That sounded flattering, not least considering that I was used to people questioning my competencies. On the whole, however, I wasn't too eager to teach, because the experience of teaching ontology engineering to the students at FUB was underwhelming to the point I was of the opinion that it would be better to leave academia. Rafael's flattery convinced me.

'From that viewpoint, I'm happy to share my knowledge with them,' I responded (someone thinks I know something of interest – yay!), 'and support the revolution and return once more to Cuba.' In my mind I continued the sentence with a 'and enjoy that academia perk of travelling for as long as it lasts and it might be a useful experience on top of it all.'

The time was set for April 2010, and it would be for some 20 postgraduate students from higher education institutions in Havana, to be held at the University of Havana. Since Cuba had limited access to the internet and to scientific literature, Rafael had asked me to put as many relevant softcopies as possible on a USB stick to share with the participants. Since I had written all those blog posts for the course at FUB already, I thought I might as well put these together into one webpage and link the referenced articles locally, as that would fall under the 'fair use' clause of copyright regulations. This compilation into one long webpage turned out to be the first substantive step towards writing the first textbook on ontology engineering for computer scientists, which eventually saw the light of day in 2018 after several intermediate extension and updates from that very preliminary version.[20]

I updated the slides and had printed them out too, to cover for an eventuality that the one data projector the department had would not be available. Rafael sorted out the logistics, with students from the University of Havana, CUJAE, and CENATAV, a classroom with a blackboard, the data projector, a fancy academic visa that ended up as a sticker in my passport, and accommodation nearby.

---

[20]For the curious: there is an open access version of the textbook available from the book's website at https://people.cs.uct.ac.za/~mkeet/OEbook/ and hardcopies published by College Publications can be bought from online bookstores. For the even more curious: It took another eight years to have the opportunity again to visit Cuba, in 2018, when I was on sabbatical and wanted to finish the first version of that textbook on ontology engineering. It provided a nice ambience to make great strides and finish the first draft: at a casa particular with a balcony, I wrote in the morning, had a short break with a Cuban salsa lesson, wrote more in the afternoon, went for a walk and dinner and then either relaxed or wrote more in the evening. No email disruptions or internet distractions, my room was cleaned, clothes washed, breakfast served, and I dined out – amazing how much time that freed up to concentrate and get work done.

Upon arrival, the tourist queue was long, it was late, and I didn't feel like queuing, so when the 'Cubans and residents etc' lines were empty, I decided to try my luck – I already had a visa and I wasn't actually a tourist. It worked! In Cuba they take an interest in tourists who show some ideological support for the revolution and the socialist project, but an academic visa for teaching a course at what was regarded as the best university in the country was a whole different category. This positive response turned out to be typical from Cubans throughout my stay. A refreshing change from Italy, where the prevailing opinion seemed to be that academics are lazy, have long holidays, and are full of *baroni*, which is the Italian variant of nepotism in academia.

The classroom was about a 30-seater, with wooden desks configured in columns either by the one desk or two desks put together, and enough computers on the desks for the participants. It was a good size venue for the around 20 postgraduate students.

After initial greetings, I mentioned to them that I was willing to try to do the lab sessions in Spanish, but preferred to do the lectures in English because I had never taught in Spanish. It's one thing to make language mistakes in a 1:1 conversation but a whole different category to screw up a lecture. There was some interaction with the students during the lectures; not a lot, but already more than the students in Italy, so I concluded I'd make it through fine.

Rafael was not convinced. Sometime during the second day, the students claimed they were confident that my command of the Spanish language would be good enough to lecture in Spanish, and they tried hard to persuade me to switch. Rafael readily concurred, and added that normally there was more interaction. I eventually gave in and promised I'd give it a try the next day. The remainder of the time, from Tuesday later that afternoon and the whole evening at the *casa particular*, I nervously practised the lecture, looking up in the hardcopy dictionary every word I didn't know the Spanish equivalent of and writing it down on the slide printouts. Hooray for printouts. Then I repeated the process as an attempt to try to remember the new vocabulary so that I would not need the 'cheat sheet' and the explanations would flow nicely.

It worked out, mostly. The main benefit of switching the lectures to Spanish was the much-increased inter-action with the students, both regarding questions and discussions about the course's content, the general under-standing of it in all likelihood too, and the rapport with the participants. This made it fun to teach – and I am still in contact with some of those students. All in all, it was a success and made me genuinely enjoy teaching. So much so, in fact, that I decided to give aiming to stay in academia – pursuing a tenured job, more precisely – a try after all. Perhaps the quiet students in Italy were the exception and the eager Cuban students were the norm, hungry for knowledge as we had been in Wageningen.

Then there's that one incident that made it work out *mostly* rather than fully. There was a slide on developing an ontology bottom-up, where you try to re-use similar resources and somehow transform them into an ontology. That fateful slide was about a rules-as-you-go approach from thesaurus to lightweight ontology; for instance, that an entry 'Milk BT Cow' should become 'Milk part of Cow', and similar for several other animals. 'Goat' was on the slide. I had looked the word up in the dictionary but hadn't written it down on the slide because of the not uncommon 'ah, yes, that word; how could I forget; sure I know this; I will remember that now'.

But, during class, in the middle of the explanation about that particular bottom-up method, I could not for the life of me remember the Spanish word for goat. I was stuck in a train of explanation that was going full speed ahead on track for a collision. As I got closer to the sentence where I was going to have to use 'goat', my thoughts grew frantic as I tried to recall 'goat' and I scrolled through in my mind for other husbandry that also gives milk that humans consume, hoping that either of the two would pop into my head at the very last second. The latter did: horses and horse milk, *leche de cavallo*! I was relieved to have found a way out. When I mentioned that as similar to the cow's milk, I saw some facial expressions change.

'We drink horse milk in the Netherlands,' I offered. 'Maybe you don't do that here, like in Ireland they don't eat horse meat and a horse isn't in fact seen in the category of animal husbandry like that.'

Some first giggles in class. That was not the response I was expecting. What's wrong with horse milk? I blamed my Spanish that must not have been clear and I tried to say the same again. First the rule, then the second example, and another attempt at reconfirming the example.

'Really, we do drink horse milk in the Netherlands. In several other countries they do too.'

One more audible giggle.

'Here we don't drink horse milk,' a male student said, shaking his head so as to non-verbally emphasise it.

I was confused now: they had understood what I tried to say, yet something was still off.

Another male student tried to help me out of my misery with a small hint. 'It holds for the other examples,' he offered, 'but horse milk is different. I don't drink that.' All the while trying to keep a straight face while the female student sitting next to him explicitly made a face indicating 'well, I sure might'.

That was worrisome. Some do and some don't. So far, the only commonality for one or the other seemed to be the students' gender. They saw on my face that something was dawning on me ...

When it became clear eventually, the class was laughing aloud and I'm sure I must have turned red from embarrassment. Consuming *leche de cavallo* means to swallow when giving a blow-job. Yeah, we do that in the Netherlands too.

That was definitely one of the more memorable mistakes I made learning another language. Those who can go about in academia in their own language have no idea how much of an advantage that is.

The rest of the course went well, still in Spanish, and there were some good mini-projects, one of which was brushed up into a good conference paper with Francis Fernandez and Annette Morales, who went on to obtain their PhDs, as did Rafael, who also visited us in Italy. I returned to Europe and started applying for jobs in academia, letting that application and initial job offer in industry fizzle out.

....

How many times can one be 'baptised' into teaching in academia? The first lecturing experiences in my first permanent job was yet a different story altogether. They had no 'sweetie ...' policy either. It was more like 'sucker, although you are tenured, you do face two years on probation so we thus can heap more onto you, because you're in no position to complain'. At least it was not the six years temping in the tenure track that is common in the USA and Europe. Let's touch upon that 'sucker ...' policy.

I never planned to work and live in South Africa, but here I was at the end of January 2011, a tenured senior lecturer and the only female academic in the computer science department at the Westville campus. As if the 'teach a brand new course' at the Fee University of Bozen-Bolzano wasn't enough practice in course design in one's early-stage career, the head of department assigned me to teach the worst course one can be assigned, whether on tenure track or tenured: theory of computation. No one receives good student evaluations teaching that, nor high pass rates with good marks. It is demanding to teach and even more demanding when enrolled in the course. At least I had attended theory of computation at FUB, which had been taught by an excellent teacher (Diego Calvanese) and there were textbooks and other materials that would help me set up the course, since the lecturers of the predecessor courses did not share their material.

I was to learn only later that I had been thrown into a hornet's nest, where the course as it was in the handbook for that year was new and a result of both what seemed to be an as of yet unresolved power play in the department and a glitch during the tenure of the previous head of department. It turned out that the course was a merger of two separate full courses of the two main components to theory of computation and both contents were largely simply copied to have a list of topics of two courses that had to be taught in the same time as one. And that in a climate where it is an imperative that all topics listed in the handbook must be covered in the course and not doing so might be seen as insubordination.

It was that same course where I had survived that mob of 15+ students who did not want to be taught by a woman (see Chapter 5).

Irrespective of the students, even if they had all been geniuses, it couldn't go well, no matter what. Indeed, it didn't run smoothly. The gentleman's agreement with management at the end of 2011 was to come to an agreement with the other lecturer at the other campus and next head of department on a reduced form, that is, verbal permission to violate an unrealistic handbook entry in the same way, and to update the handbook accordingly to have something sensible for 2013 onward. But gentleman's agreements don't work when there's a reorganisation and a power grab by a different faction. Sayre's law comes to mind, which states that 'Academic politics is the most vicious and bitter form of politics, because the stakes are so low', as quoted in the *Wall Street Journal* as early as 20 December 1973 and repeated in variants many times over. I'll spare you the details.

There was some writing on the wall and I was supposed to have taken up the earlier advice from my 'induction officer' which he had so generously shared with me in 2011. As with any new job, I hedged my bets and socialised with everyone in the department and around it – choosing sides in whatever political fights may be going on can always be done later, if needed. Of course I knew about South African history, had read up some more, and I had noticed a few cracks in Potemkin village when I had visited South Africa in 2008 and 2010 for a researcher exchange, but none of this prepared me for how complicated things can be and just how much apartheid has messed with people's minds.

And so it came to be one day in early May that I was having a chat with a well-meaning colleague, let's call him Divesh, who served as the induction officer of sorts and felt it his kind-hearted duty to explain a few things to me. We were standing outside on the landing of the computer science floor of the building taking a break from work, with a view on the car park and the building on the other side.

'You're new here in South Africa,' he commenced. 'I'll tell you how things really work here, in South Africa in general and at the university in particular. It seems you have not caught up on that yet.'

As I'm not one not willing to listen to whatever advice people want to share with me, I didn't object and non-verbally indicated he could continue.

'You know about the different races we have here,' he went on. 'There are the blacks. No need to talk about them, right, we can set them aside. Then there are coloureds. There are hardly any here in this part of the country, as they mostly live in the Western Cape, so we can ignore them too.'

I tried my best to not intervene and let him show the back of his tongue to see where this train of argument was heading. And anyway, he gave me no opportunity to interrupt.

Divesh continued, 'Then, then it gets interesting. You might think Indians, but no, then come the whites. We can't set them aside and we have to deal with them, including foreigners like you. Some are okay, and smart even. But it is Indians who are on top.'

Still not saying anything, I grimaced that I wasn't with him on why, or how, he had arrived at the pecking order and his supposed conclusion. Unperturbed, he continued with thinking he was providing me a service explaining how society worked and he added a bit more explanation for dubious measure.

'You'd agree that Indians and whites can do things equally well with no inherent differences, right?' he said, to which I nodded yes, 'but ...' – he paused for dramatic effect, and then continued with a smile and tone of voice to share his epiphany – 'we've had it much harder than the whites, and yet performing equal, so that actually makes us better!'

I raised my eyebrows at that, after which he toned it down slightly, although still not permitting interruptions.

'Okay, yeah, we possibly can't say *all* Indians, and there are still the Indians who worked at UDW [the university for South African Indians during apartheid], but those of us who worked at UND [the university for white South Africans during apartheid] after apartheid, we, we really *are* better than the whites.'

'Uhm,' I started, in an attempt to buy some time to think about how to respond to this sort of argument. The only experience I had had was about rebutting twisted arguments to explain why whites weren't *Übermenchen*, not why Indians weren't superior either. But I had no chance. My induction officer of sorts, supposedly being a superior being and all, was so generous as to continue yet further to explain to me the consequences of this particular hierarchy straight away.

'To get along,' he said, I had to acknowledge that 'Indians are on top, especially the ones from the former

UND, and you have to please us to have a sliver of a chance to get ahead.'

My jaw dropped when Divesh said that. He is supposedly intrinsically better and I have to acknowledge this profusely and repeatedly?

'Uh, I have to kiss the asses especially of the ex-UND Indians, you say, rather than first getting to know everyone since I'm new here?' I managed to ask to see if he truly meant what he was saying and I had understood him correctly.

'Yes,' he confirmed, 'and if you do that long and well enough, then maybe, just maybe, you might get ahead.'

It went on a little further, where he advised that I shouldn't be hanging out anymore with the ex-UDW Indians and the few blacks that occasionally dropped by, as that would not be good for my career. At some point, I half-heartedly excused myself, saying that I should be returning to work, and walked away. There was no convincing him otherwise anyway, nor much chance to derail his monologue and start rebutting. I did not take that advice, since I did then, and still do, think that all humans are created equal and that conviction is neither up for negotiation nor up for sale, and several individuals working harder to obtain the same does not make a whole race (or sex/gender, for that matter) superior. I associated with whomever I got along with, and it is those people at that workplace who gave me lasting good memories. And, indeed, that opinion and attitude did not help me advance in the organisation, and in due time I left for greener pastures.

The speech was shocking to me, but it did put into better context many of my experiences in the city. A twisted silver lining, if it can be called that, was that I gained experience about what racism feels like at the receiving end, which was a valuable lesson, albeit not one I wish to repeat or have more of. At work, it meant a so-called double whammy: having to put up with what is commonly considered to be both sexism and racism (and an occasional sprinkling of xenophobia, it seemed). Just one of these is more than enough to put up with.

Suffice it to say that the whole saga and everything to do with it was a very unpleasant learning moment regarding the worth of a gentleman's agreement (zero) and what an intentionally hostile baptism into academia can look like – yet to be smart and strong enough to stay standing, learn some labour law along the way, and reflect on messy politics in academia and in South Africa. To those who caused the problem in the first place before I arrived, who concocted this sort of set-up, supported it, supported those who enacted or supported it, and, as if that was not enough, had no qualms about making students collateral damage to boot due to, in my opinion, a distorted, narrow-minded, and short-sighted worldview and politics: shame on you. If your university has a 'sucker ...' practice, my advice is: leave. As soon as possible or even before that. Those who think exploiting probationers or tenure-trackers is acceptable and good for a laugh are uncollegial and they will not turn into good colleagues once you're confirmed or have obtained tenure. Don't let it, and them, ruin your life. It's their loss.

....

It is well known in academia that if you want to push someone out of the system, you assign them some more administrative tasks, heap more teaching onto them, or make them teach an 'awful' course that will inevitably result in you receiving a low evaluation from students whose feedback are, all too often, still taken into consideration with regard to tenure and promotion. For computer science, that's assigning someone to teach a theory of computation course. Someone's got to do it, though.

With sabbaticals and teaching buy-out of the colleagues who typically teach it, in 2021 it's my turn again. With the current winds blowing, ever more stressed and anxious students, ever increasing teaching load, more students, and more administration, and theory of computation being what it is, I would be wise to make a plan B again, even while tenured.

13

NO WOMEN IN COMPUTER SCIENCE

The Stage: 2010–2020 – Italy, The Netherlands

Jokes by email aside, the jobs in the IT industry feel like a bygone era, 'so last century' in what was acceptable behaviour then and now. If sexist jokes were to be emailed to the team on a regular basis now, the minimum would be a trip to HR and likely suspension. Assimilation or blending in and also not rocking the boat is still very much the way to go, though – if you get in, that is. One may split hairs or chop logic over the fact that computer science, computer engineering, information systems and information technology are all different disciplines, but not rocking any boats still holds, at least for computer science, engineering and IT, and assimilation holds for any jobs, including academic ones.[21]

Let me start with the first motivation for the title of this chapter. We're in the computer science faculty building at the Free University of Bozen-Bolzano, on the second floor, left corridor, which has a number of offices. Associate and full professors each have their own office, two researchers

---

[21] I will not recount too much in this or the next chapter, for the repercussions it may have as a member of the scientific community. At least I have tenure and there are still publication venues that have a double-blind peer-review process where the names of both the reviewers and authors of a submitted manuscript are hidden. Yet, I would not want the situation where colleagues wouldn't want to interact with me for fear of ending up in a memoir. Do not worry: I have no plan to write another one.

share one office, and PhD students are put together in an open-plan office. One day, there was a small celebration of something in one of the professors' offices. I can't recall the reason – a birthday or project awarded or something like that – but it came with snacks and drinks and the room was crowded with research group members. One of the researchers was a charming, elegantly dressed and well-educated young man. He was slimly built and maybe his talking and posturing was intended to make up for that, or maybe that's what Italians are like anyhow, as the culture in the south – that is, anywhere south of Trentino Alto Adige/Trient und Süd Tirol – is rather different from that up north in Bolzano in the Alps, where I worked. It remains a mystery. At this modest celebration, he was in one of his storytelling and boasting moods, which were generally entertaining to listen to. At some point in the story, he was gesticulating with a typical arm-hand movement where the hand moves up, turns slightly inward, with fingers spreading a bit, face slightly tilted forward with a stern look as precursor to communicate something deep. He stated:

'*Non ci sono le donne in informatica; ci sono essere umani col sesso femminile.*' There are no women in computer science; there are human beings who are of the female sex.

I stared in disbelief, rewinding the story a little in my head in an attempt to try to replay and parse that sentence again to check whether I had misunderstood it the first time round. Surely I had? No. I looked around and saw another assistant professor, her body rigid from anger and eyes wide. Our gazes met, very much agreeing on a *WTF just happened! Are we going to say something about this or not?* But the conversation had moved on already and the opportune moment to interrupt had passed. As if such statements were the order of the day, and life continues.

Not even human beings of the female sex can get into the research group, other than in temping jobs. At some day around 2010, we were having lunch in the university's cafeteria with one of the generally quiet PhD students and my official former PhD supervisor, who hadn't done much positive advising or supervising other than urging me to put more logic and proofs in my draft thesis, emailing his gastronomic itinerary of Rome, and providing additional project money for travel to conferences so that I could present my peer-reviewed published papers all around the world. The topic of jobs and appointments came up.

He was so generous to share with us academic young-sters that, as a rule, they didn't hire women for tenured jobs. Widening my eyes and raising my eyebrows, I asked why not.

'They go off having babies and take too much time off on maternity leave, which then means more work for us on our shoulders, and so it's *de facto* a vacated place that we cannot afford to lose.'

One of the ladies in administration was indeed doing something resembling that by strategically timing several pregnancies and therewith being mostly away for four years and counting. He mentioned this lady to illustrate his point.

'But,' I started to counter, 'only very few women will take that much time off and plan it in that way, especially academics, and many don't want to have kids, even. And so you cannot assume that upfront we're all out to game the system to try to secure a full salary while only procreating. We don't study for a PhD to then become full-time moms. And look at our colleague who was effectively on paternity leave for several months.'

The PhD student was listening in like a child tries to overhear their parents' conversation and in no way daring to interrupt or to add his two cents. My former supervisor continued unfazed.

'But he's different,' he said, 'it's not the same. And yeah, okay, you may be the exception that then might be considered.'

There was little point in arguing further – that I was not an exception – without the evidence in hand. Looking at the women alumni who temped at the research group I was a member of, they are either still temping in academia, have tenure or work in industry, with zero or more children, and succeeding fine. No full-time moms. Two new tenured posts have been filled in the meantime, both by men, and statistically there are at least some 80% men in that field of specialisation, if not 90%, so statistically they are not that much off.

Maybe he did not even provide a disservice expressing his point of view: how many think it but do not say it? With that being said, quite frankly, neither do I appreciate uncollegial colleagues who hoist their teaching and admi-nistration obligations on me and the rest of the department. In the case of the prof's feared predicament, rather than blocking potential 'maternity escapees', the system should change. As a minimum, there should be paid replacement teaching during the maternity/paternity leave period, if only because punishing those who choose not to spend their time raising young children in the nuclear family is not conducive to collegiality and, as it turns out, not conducive to academic job prospects for women.

Should you apply for a job opening if they, or any other

male-only department, have an opening even if you're not going to make it because of an unwritten policy on gendered hiring practices? Yes, definitely. If women don't even bother to apply, if they throw in the towel before the game has even started, men like him will think there are no women in the candidate pool to choose from. Additionally, if you happen to be in a hostile environment, don't be discouraged completely: there are teams and departments that are less hostile and possibly even welcoming. The next paragraph doesn't describe one of those, however.

....

When living abroad, every once in a while you become fed up being the foreigner – it happens to me; it happens to everyone. It may be due to some last straw after a sequence of administrative obstacles of rules-for-foreigners, a cultural difference you stumbled hard over, the desire to go ice-skating on a frozen pond once more, or a fleeting craving for, say, *borrelnootjes* or *stroopwafels*. It's not that you'd want to go back to the country of origin for good, but fewer hassles and *faux pas* can sound appealing occasionally. The feeling typically goes as quickly as it arrives.

In one of those moments in 2012, while I was employed as a senior lecturer in South Africa, an advertisement passed by for a lecturer position at the Department of Computer Science at the Technical University in Eindhoven (TU/e), which is located about 16 km from the village where I grew up. It was a rank lower than I was employed at, but it's a better university, so it still could be an improvement. Should I apply? I pondered. I could remember the chemistry department tour from secondary school and, while they presumably had done their best, somehow it had not felt particularly inviting. Additionally, I certainly had not forgotten the dismal numbers from the background research of a blog post I wrote a few years before about women in STEM[22]: TU/e had 1.6% female professors; 2 out of 127. I decided I wanted to give it a try nonetheless. I had looked at the profiles of the other lecturers in the department, and for sure my CV was about as good as theirs and in some cases better. If I were to end up in the 'not a good fit' basket eventually, then at least I'd have had a paid trip to visit my brother and his family, since I assumed I would make it to the shortlist at least.

I wasn't even shortlisted. Tsk!

The rejection letter did not bother to state the reason(s). Now I do know a few basics of Dutch labour law and so I knew I had the right to ask for an explanation why, which, by law, they then have to provide. So I requested an explanation and, I presumed, let them sweat on it. They outsmarted me on that one. I received a response stating that, indeed, it wasn't that my achievements weren't good enough, but they were looking for an appropriate fit for that specific role where the candidate had the right amount of achievements, not too few but not too many either. Put differently: supposedly, I was overqualified. Overqualified in academia!

That's perhaps a world-wide first – yay me.

Legally in Dutch law, rejection due to overqualification is a legitimate reason for denying someone a job: when only boring conformity with mere execution is asked for, overqualified people start rocking the boat; and they move

---

[22]https://keet.wordpress.com/2010/08/13/south-african-women-on-leadership (last checked on 4 September 2021).

on to greener pastures too quickly to recuperate the costs of the hiring process. We all know overqualification is just never the real reason in the hiring processes in academia. However, spending an inordinate amount of time proving this in court was not worth my time although, to me, it was a fine example of how one can keep women out of the system.

When I told this story later at a social dinner of a workshop in charming Galway, Ireland, when the topic of finding jobs in academia came up, as it invariably did because the market is tough, a colleague from the continental part of Europe offered two possible alternative reasons.

'I know they are illegal,' he began, 'but you hear things through the grapevine that it has happened occasionally. I don't know where though ...' (protecting himself). Everyone participating in the conversation understood – certain happenings in academia can be fed into the grapevine, but not any particular details. He continued, intending to kindly provide some insider knowledge from said grapevine. 'They may have had an anointed one for the appointment and then the ad would have been for form only; or they knew that this tenure-track post was never going to materialise into the permanent post it is supposed to lead to so you aim for a mediocre one who won't have to be confirmed.'

I had heard of the former as well, but not the latter. As to what it may have been? Take your pick. I still lean towards sexism being alive and thriving as the more probable explanation, because of the dismal gender balance at the TU/e.

....

Fast-forward 10 years from aforementioned women in STEM data. It didn't improve a lot at the TU/e, but by 2019 they had woken up to the fact that, indeed, actually, there were rather few female academics. Gosh. Better late than never, one might think.

My brother sent me a screenshot of an article in the hard copy of the regional newspaper, dated 18 June 2019, which announced TU/e's plan to address it: from 1 July 2019 all job ads for academic personnel would be open only to women for the next 1.5 years; thereafter, they expected that the posts would be open again for both women and men as they would have by then increased the percentage to 20% female professors.

My brother was impressed; shocked, it seemed, even. To sidestep men and advantage women in that manner! This surely would please me? No. I almost could see his head-shake coming through in the text message: the university had made a major policy decision, yet still it wasn't good enough. Still I was complaining. The worst of it was in the first sentence of the article.

'De technische universiteit wil vrouwen het liefst voor een periode voor vijf jaar aanstellen.'

The technical university would prefer to hire women on a five-year contract.

Come again?! No! Give us those jobs with tenure that we deserve, with a permanent position, like you did with the boys in the boys' club. Why should I even want to try to go for such a crumb of a temping gig when lesser qualified men are awarded with tenure? That's not fair and the plan stinks.

What that decision by its top management amounts to is an attempt at short-term massaging of a bad state of affairs so as to look less bad at the bean-counting date, not a genuine attempt at structural change. If I had studied computer science in the Netherlands straight out of secondary school (say, 5 years to MSc + 4 years PhD) to only be offered such a crumb for employment another 18 years later, I would have left the field years ago. No one keeps on going under the condition of sexism and perpetual temping in a way that you can't speak up about it. If a woman survives in computer science, rest assured she's not a doormat and she is not someone given to waiting patiently.

Female academics in science at universities in South Africa complain – and we do have reasons to complain – but it's all relative and it's not nearly as bad as in the Netherlands. Here, women are hired and receive tenure, even if the percentages are progressively less due to a leaking pipeline. There are about 20-25% female academics, which many science departments and universities in the Netherlands don't even come close to. For all the problems that South Africa has, the country has ample experience, and a plethora of ways, when it comes to trying to redress the injustices of the past. They may not achieve the theoretically optimal results, but they are more effective than TU/e's stunt.

While I'm clearly not a refugee, one could argue that in some sense I've taken refuge in a place that is less hostile to women in science than my 'home country'. Further, as was the case during the Celtic Tiger and IT boom in Ireland, South Africa has a skills shortage in IT and computing, so they don't mind too much (and, in fact, are actively recruiting) that the applicants are not in the white male category.

As to TU/e and the other two technical universities and the agricultural one: Dutch Baby Boomers heading for retirement is a golden opportunity to push for some demographic changes. And perhaps COVID-19 will contribute to make it a real shortage of computer science academics, so that there's no option but to look beyond the boys' club. It would be rather sad if that might, or were to be, the only way to have that lot be taught a lesson to take a stride towards equality, but it wouldn't be the first time: it took women's work during World War I to obtain the vote.

The alternative, a setback where the modest gains of the past 20 years are undone due to COVID-19, is, unfortunately also a possible scenario, due to the increased burden of care that interferes with scoring the principal currencies of research brownie points. Preliminary research suggests this may be the case[23], as if the pandemic is a return-to-start chance card in a game of Monopoly right when you had made it through paying rent for a few costly streets with hotels.

---

[23]An introductory article about the issues, with links to the research, can be found at, among others: Keymanthri Moodley and Amanda Gouws. How women in academia are feeling the brunt of COVID-19. The Conversation, 7 August 2020. online: https://theconversation.com/how-women-in-academia-are-feeling (last accessed on 30 May 2021). Also, data suggests it affects mainly women with care responsibilities, especially for small children: T. Murat Yildirim and Hande Eslen-Ziya. The differential impact of COVID-19 on the work conditions of women and men academics during the lockdown. Gender, Work & Organization, 2021, 28(S1): 243–249. The one exception I could find was an analysis for the six academic journals of the British Ecological Society, where they had not observed a gendered impact (unlike in the many papers they cite where it is so): Charles W. Fox and Jennifer Meyer, The influence of the global COVID-19 pandemic on manuscript submissions and editor and reviewer performance at six ecology journals. Functional Ecology, 2021, 35(1):4-10.

14

I HAVE IMPORTANT
THINGS TO DO

The Stage: 2010s – South Africa; elsewhere, too

Let's modify that teaching plan again. Update those slides. Carry out more research and write more articles. Write another grant proposal for a funding call with 5-10% acceptance rate. The committee is looking for members, especially from under-represented groups. Also on repeat: do read the course notes and announcements, dear students, as your lecturer or convenor is not an automated question-answering system. Students are taught and some of them inspired, papers are published, projects accepted, and service contributed. And so on and so forth; slog and toil, shut up and do it; more of it is better. The mid-career slump is somewhere between the promise of a bright scientific future that a freshly minted PhD graduate has and having enough grey hair and wrinkles to pass for seasoned senior academic looking to be at least in your mid/late 50s. I can still count my few grey hairs and wrinkles, and have a few years left to reach 50. Even if one has made it this far, that mid-career still does not come with less gender-directed weirdness, but the skin is thicker.

A disclaimer upfront, and trying to duck while I'm at it – those self-defeating upfront apologies that try to avoid upsetting anyone, which we're told not to do – before we jump straight into it. Perhaps I'm treading on ever thinner ice with the contents of this chapter. The anecdotes recounted here, however, are not meant to take a stab at one colleague or another specifically (also in this chapter, some names have been changed to protect people's identities). There are many instances that can be recounted. I have chosen the ones that follow because they are illustrative and typical and can be recounted more concisely in one connected arc. They are not isolated events, however.

Be this as it may, popular media, 'quit-lit' articles about leaving academia and similar writings might categorise the anecdotes as microaggressions, systemic or not. I don't think they were intended as premeditated acts of aggression. What I'm describing is just part of the run-of-the-mill interactions in the workplace, but maybe I give people too much benefit of the doubt.

Much the same as most colleagues, I did not receive my promotion the first time I applied for it at my current employer. Gossip goes around why, which I'll leave for what it is, except for one general comment: *labor omnia vincit* (hard work conquers all), it is said, which I assumed for a long while to be true, but which is definitely not the case. The second autocomplete suggestion to typing 'academia is not' in Google's search box, is 'a meritocracy'. Go figure. Anyway, when that rejection happens to you, you can ask for a meeting with the dean to ask about reasons for the refusal, as a gentleman's version of the request-by-law I mentioned in the previous chapter. So I did. Not that gentlemen things are worth anything for non-gentlemen, but to satisfy my curiosity for a fresh anecdote and to carve another line on the *ishango* (tally stick). The dean at the time was a very tall and old-school English white South African. I don't know if what he told me was his own opinion or the majority or the consensus view of the promotion evaluation committee. Regardless, the first and main reason was my research record, of all things, of which he had the audacity to claim utter ignorance.

'We don't know what the main venues are in your field of specialisation,' he said, 'but we know you're not publishing in them.'

I was too taken aback with such nonsense to actually respond properly, other than some muttering that I had multiple papers in main venues, which I do. Unlike, say, the effectiveness of teaching, which is difficult to measure in praxis, research output is the one and only component of the promotion application documentation that can easily be looked up and assessed. The evidence is there, with numerous papers in the well-respected A- and B-rated conferences.

The committee might as well put a commemoration plaque on the wall: 'If you can't find fault, then you have to invent it'.

The promotion application evaluation committee is one of those faculty-wide committees, which as such has no clue about my field of specialisation; a bit like how a regular computer scientist won't know much about the ins and outs of other fields of specialisation in science. I was also advised to change referees, since they supposedly had not been positive about me, according to the dean/ the committee. Of course, the latter comment generated a nagging thought: was it perhaps backstabbing referees that was the problem, or was the committee actually trying to drive a wedge between us and invent another excuse? The former seemed unlikely but I enquired with those referees and they claimed it was not them. One of them said he had written that it 'would have been better if you had had more papers in A-rated conferences', which was true, but that is true for everyone, and to spin that as 'no A-rated' venue papers is still factually false. Besides, spinning that as the main reason merely is, at best, suggestive of the indication of the committee's poverty of adequate expertise to judge. Practically, there was no recourse. I was not the first women in the science faculty this happened to and definitely have not been the last one either. Let's hope that the transformation that is being talked about so much will extend to gender and promotion processes too.

A male colleague knowledgeable about the particular promotion application process for that year, let's call him Prof Khan, indicated another take on it from his viewpoint, also apparently knowing no depths to inventing excuses to twist interpretation of facts a certain way.

'Not all A-rated conferences are equal,' he began, 'and some of them are more really A than others.' That was the first part of this argument, while we were having a chat in the hallway of a building on campus, although he was making the assertion in a different context where another male colleague was taking a 'research week break' right before the start of the academic year to finalise a paper for a top publication venue. The conversation was insightful, however, in that this very easily could have been part of the promotion assessment deliberations when it came to me. Prof Khan continued with his argument defending the research break: 'It is hard to get into the A-rated publication venue in FabScienceField' (... and we should bend over backwards to grant him that time, was the implied communication between the lines).

I replied that it is hard to have papers accepted in any A-rated publication venue. That it requires a lot of work since it's at the level of relatively ground-breaking rather than good incremental science. I said I knew this because I had some experience there.

'No, it is *really hard* to get into those A-rated venues,' he tried to explain to me – I guess 'mansplain' is the applicable term nowadays. He went on to needle a bit more in a tone that he was trying to get something through to that presumably near-empty skull of mine. 'It is so hard to get into that he only managed to have papers accepted there once he collaborated with colleagues from outside the university!'

In other words, that I had had papers accepted in A-rated conferences as main author must mean that those were 'lesser A' conferences, this supported by the fact that I hadn't leeched onto an external-to-UCT 'bigshot' author – since I could not possibly be a 'bigshot' author in my own right, with whom other people may want to collaborate to have a paper accepted at an A-rated conference.

Jeez!

The thought that I actually may be creative and smart enough to pull off relatively remarkable science not just once but several times to having those papers accepted in A-rated scientific publication venues, and even be awarded a Best Paper Award at an A-rated conference, was inconceivable to him. Just because someone finds it implausible, does not mean it is impossible. If there was any bright side to this at all, it was that at least now I knew his viewpoint more explicitly. The time to walk away and do some more research, regardless of what he thought of it, was overdue.

I am not going to give too many of those examples, lest someone wants to add them to their repertoire of trying to belittle and put down colleagues. Besides, besmirching venue classifications is not a common strategy to try to drag down an academic. The more common approach is to question contributions, since that is much harder to determine from the outside than all those conference ranking lists that roughly agree with one another. There's a list of authors on an article, but that does not necessarily give away who contributed the most work or had the crucial insight, and who had a near-free ride, if anyone. The order of authors on a scientific article also depends on the (sub)discipline, so that may not reveal enough. Common orders are students first and head of the lab last, by order of contribution, or alphabetically by surname. Most of the papers that I'm an author of follows either of the last two options. Sometimes the order of contribution turns out to be alphabetically by surname along with it, as is often the case with my linguist collaborator, whereas with another collaborator we switched from order of contribution to alphabetical order after a few years. Anyhow, if you haven't been in the kitchen seeing the research being prepared, cooked and served, such matters are unclear from a distance.

The article I receive dubious comments about most often is the one published at the A-rated International Conference on Knowledge Representation and Reasoning in 2008. The authors are listed in alphabetical order by surname, which means I'm last in line after two well-known and widely respected scientists.

'I thought they only added you to be nice,' a few colleagues have said by now already.

'You mean like a charity case?' I rub on a little.

'Yeah,' comes the typical response.

'No!' follows. A resounding no.

Actually, it was my insight and I wrote a large part of the paper. Alessandro mainly improved the proofs and was corresponding author just in case I'd screwed that up, notwithstanding I'd been doing it successfully for years already; and Nicola, to put it in terms of one of my former students, mainly 'pimped up the paper' to give it momentum in a broader context. We all contributed such that it helped get the paper accepted. A charity case I most certainly was not.

I travelled to Sydney to present the paper at the conference. The session I was to present in was situated in a large classroom where the chairs were lined up in rows to seat about 50 or so attendees, all of them academics, from PhD students to senior professors from across the world, but with white male academics the overwhelming majority. As with each presentation, there were 15 minutes to present the key aspects of the paper and then there were five minutes for questions and answers. Right from the start of the question and answer session, I was heckled by a highly esteemed professor. He had a paper on a different aspect of the broad area that we used to solve the problem and he wanted me to admit that his paper was more relevant and more important than mine. Academia can be like a kindergarten sandbox at times. I tried to respond nicely and politely.

'Your paper is on a different subtopic and possibly could indeed be of interest at a later stage when one may want to proceed to scalable implementations, but we first wanted to thoroughly solve the problem without constraints upfront. Now we know what's needed, and that then can inform how to optimise it in some way accordingly.'

My explanation was to no avail. The esteemed professor kept at it, repeating himself with another so-called question that was rhetorical at best: 'But would you not agree with me that [those things in our paper] should have been important considerations from the outset?'

No, again, and shut up now was the response that crossed my mind, and which might have been readable from my facial expression or non-verbal communication. My co-author Alessandro was also in attendance and he eventually intervened by sighing loudly and saying bluntly, 'No, come on, this is off topic, leave it' and that it was as I said. That made the esteemed professor stop, letting out a final little grumbling that he was not happy he hadn't got us to agree and admit his paper to be more important.

Frankly, by then I couldn't care less. I was all the way on the other side of the globe, in Sydney! Of course I had not heeded my own mental note from Cuba on not taking time off before a scientific conference and I had gladly embraced the conference organisers' advice to come a day or two earlier to adjust to the huge time zone difference. In that extra acclimatisation time, I had finally checked off realising a daydream I had had long ago in the 1991/92 school year. We had been covering modern architecture in the arts history class and the lecturer had put up a slide of the Sydney Opera House. While he was explaining the deeper artsy aspects of it, I was thinking and promising myself *Ah, I will travel and make it to the other end of the world and see this myself in person.* And I did. Not as a self-paid tourist, but paid for by the university because I was presenting a paper as main author at a top scientific conference in the field. Hah! Nobody can take that away from me. I took a photo from the Sydney Opera House, printed it, and framed it. To this day, it hangs on the wall at home.

The impact of the contents of the paper? There is no scalable implementation of the logic used, nor will there be due to insurmountable limitations on computational complexity, and a simplified version is too much dressed down to be of interest for automated reasoning for that problem. It still does give a valid explanation and therewith guidance in modelling part-whole relations. The most recent use citation, that is, not a mention and not a self-citation, is one of those nice pat-on-the-back ones where the authors took it as solid input to build upon for their own purposes 10 years hence: 'In accordance with [7] status classes modeling ...' where '[7]' is our paper. And it has reached a different subject domain than our toy examples of severing a boxer's hand and humans that cannot be brain-less: it is used in modelling financial reporting on a shared ledger like Blockchain.[24]

Hah!

....

A-rated and more higher truly A-rated, important and importanter; one can make up words and *ad hoc* comparisons for convenience sake so they lean in one's favour and to not be in discord with one's prejudices. Academia is not a meritocracy and not to everyone's liking. Even in academia with tenure and job scarcity, there's still

---

[24]The full reference: Blums, I. and Weigand, H. Financial Reporting by a Shared Ledger. FOMI: Formal Ontologies Meet Industry, Proceedings of the Joint Ontology Workshops 2017. CEUR-WS vol 2050. Bozen-Bolzano, Italy, September 21–23, 2017. http://ceur-ws.org/Vol-2050/.

a high turnover rate in computing, although not as high as in industry. Colleagues come and go and we try to make newcomers feel welcome and explain things more here and there to get them up to speed, because that's what anyone appreciates arriving new at a job.

And so it was this one time, but the newcomer was not doing much of the administration tasks he was supposed to be doing. So I did some of those if it was urgent, and let him know he was supposed to have been doing a particular task (that was his job), which would have prevented the extra work. At some point, students had figured out I was responsive but my colleague was not, notwithstanding that I sent them to him to have their issues resolved. They returned to me, claiming he wasn't responding. Other students were afraid of him and wanted to try with me first so that they could avoid him altogether. All this extra work was at a time when I had my very busy months – 70 to 80 hours effective working hours per week (that is, not clocking the breaks) compared to the regular 60 hours – so it was rather unpleasant. Things reached a point when I had totally had enough of him not doing his designated administrative tasks. I walked down the corridor to his office and told him in no uncertain terms that *he* was supposed to be doing those tasks, not me, and that I would not do a single one more, even if it meant the admin task collapsed.

'Yes,' he said, and he nodded his head, to emphasise it non-verbally, 'I know.' And then, changing the expression on his face to show that he knew I was well aware of his activities, leaning forward a little over his desk toward me for further emphasis, he said: 'I had important things to do.'

As if I could not possibly have anything important to do, or in principle not ever as important as his important things. I try to be welcoming to a newcomer and some snotty sexist snub is the thank you I get!

The next generation – come to think of it: the one that my generation raised – does not give the impression of being more emancipated. I've had several postgraduate students in my office who are supervised by a male colleague, asking me for a favour. In a similar busy period around the same time, one of those PhD students, Kobena, knocked on my open office door.

'Can I interrupt you for a bit?' he asked, doing exactly that already.

I looked up from my screen and turned my head to the right in the direction of the door to indicate I had noticed him.

'Could you please have a look at my draft proposal?' Kobena asked.

'As staff, we normally don't interfere in the supervision of a colleague's student, and even if I were to give feedback on it, it may not be the most useful because your topic is definitely not in my research area,' I responded. And then: 'So you really have to ask you supervisor or co-supervisor, but not me.'

Unswerving, he continued, 'You know of the topic, and my supervisor, you know, he's really busy, very busy.'

'And you think I am not busy?!' I replied in a tone that had a whiff of irritation wafting through it.

'Uhm, well, probably yes, but you don't *look* as busy as my supervisor. Can you please have a look at it?'

'I am, and no, I won't.' I was in a sort of neutral mood, so I added a further clarification. 'Just because I may not radiate busy-ness does not mean I'm merely doodling in my office waiting to serve students who are passing by.'

Kobena's face turned into an expression that indicated he was mulling over that possibility. After a little while, he decided that that was possible. He apologised for the interruption and, disappointed, he left.

There is no specific profile of undergraduate and postgraduate students who knock on my door to ask if I can read some written material or explain something of another course that I do not even teach, or explain some research topic that they ought to have asked their supervisor about. Except for those students who interrupt to ask where the departmental reception is or if they can borrow my stapler. Those ones are most definitely too darn lazy and they ought not to be students at the university. They ought to walk those five metres down the hallway to the secretariat, be it for the administrative matter they have or to use that stapler if they have forgotten their own one and had forgotten to staple their papers earlier before hand-in. Besides, hard copies?!

The work of an academic is relatively autonomous. We can see 'outputs' of evidence of work done, including someone attending a meeting, showing up for one's teaching obligations, and growing one's list of publications. There are many other activities, such as student supervision, service to the research community such as organising conferences and article reviewing, project proposal writing and management, outreach activities, entertaining interrupting students and staff who think I couldn't possibly be busy, and so on, that are harder to estimate how busy all that makes a colleague. Just because you don't see all those activities does not mean we're not doing anything or that what we're doing can't possibly be as important as your own obligations because you don't happen to be the centre of it. I have important things to do too. It doesn't become worth any less when it is a woman who carries out the research, manages the project, teaches the course, or obtains the degree. The earlier everyone realises that, the better. Meanwhile, *a luta continua*.

AFTERWORD AND ACKNOWLEDGEMENTS

I hope you found peeking into the kitchen of an academic worth your time, even if at the end it turned out different from what you may have expected. Many scenic and ugly detours have been omitted, and some people may feel left out for the events omitted. There's much more to my life than these events recounted, indeed, but they're either less relevant to how I ended up as a professor in computer science – which is the story I set out to write – or relevant but not equally easy to recount into a readable tale with relatively little scene-setting and background knowledge. There are also many other stories – about parties, dancing, travels and much more – and they are more suitable for the vast body of oral history or safely left to keep gathering dust. The ones retold here were relevant in different ways, from the various types of obstructions to motivations to forge ahead nonetheless to events that left a lasting impression while travelling the bumpy road.

I hope to have given you a glimpse of those obstacles and exemplars of oddities along the road to professorship, lifting the veil a bit to peek into the academic kitchen. Other professors will have other typical stories they may think I have missed. Some of the many other topics are death by committee, the politics of titles, the dearth of mentors and advocates, and backstabbing students who run off to male academics to double-check the answer I gave them. Or about speaking up but only being noticed when you have turned it up a few notches to the academic equivalent of yelling, to then be told you're overreacting, or, more broadly, the 'crazy/bitch' narrative[25] where senior women academics are supposedly 'off' in their behaviour. At least there were no equivalents to some of the sordid stories I have read about, like on incessant harassment in the workplace, sex for grades, or sabotage of scientific experiments.

Every now and then I do ponder giving up – let the nasty people win and cease 'wasting' my time further with the 'game'. Life is too short. If it comes to that, I hope that at least in the meanwhile I have managed to inspire a few people who may be able to go further with fewer obstacles than I and most of my predecessors have had, and still put up with, by virtue of me and fellow female academics having trudged and tramped and plodded and paced around, flattening the weeds in the field here and there.

Conversely, some academics have had a comparatively comfortable ride; any minority most likely has not. It's not – or should not be – a pissing game of who had the most or the worst obstacles, but a co-operative game where in the not too distant future, Academistan with its inhabitants will be just and fair and an exemplary microcosm.

....

This afterword section is, perhaps, also the place to write a polite muttering about the English language. I'll try to keep it short. I had already admitted that I disliked the language from the very first lesson, notwithstanding some gems of prose I've read over the years. If it were a beauty contest, English would be last in line of all the languages that I have

---

[25]http://jberdahl.blogspot.com/2017/07/the-crazybitch-narrative-about-html (last accessed on 27 February 2021).

learned so far – and I've learned more than a handful of them. In the light of language use data internationally, English is currently the winner as *lingua franca* and, locally, it is the 'language of business' (crowding out the 10 other official languages of South Africa that are not the 'language of business'); hence, there seems to be no good way around it when you work across the globe. And so this book was written in English rather than in my mother tongue.

For this book in particular, a few notes may be in order. While I do get the point that the sentences had to be shorter than in my average academic writings, this cutting up into a few words per sentence isn't my preference. In case you felt offended: I did not mean to insult you, dear reader. Of course, the dearth of long sentences in this book also has to do with the fact that the English language has, comparatively to the other languages I have learned at least, quite flimsy grammar rules, which are otherwise useful crutches in grammatically richer languages since they keep more words coherently together in a larger unit of thought without running into disambiguation issues. Certain edits to some of the paragraphs make it feel like it's only just barely my voice. But they did improve the computed readability metrics scores, so there's that.

Then there's the concept of 'house style', which all academics have tales about for their scientific articles accepted for publication; it's the same story for publishing a book. Or take the Oxford comma; let it be known that I wholeheartedly agree with its use, for all the reasons raised in support of it. I can go on about all this for quite some time. Writing this book has led me to interesting nuggets of information about the English language and descend into detours with deliberations on whether the Web – the

World Wide Web sort of web, that is – may be lowercased by now thanks to its ubiquity, to name but two things. Not to mention anecdotes that count as 'learning moments' while learning the language on the job throughout the years. I'll leave that and my reflections on a language's grammar, orthography, and style, perchance, for another time.

....

I would like express my gratitude to Sharleen, who read an earlier draft, and thank Gill Leggat for useful and encouraging feedback on chapters one and seven. Many thanks are also due to David and Gail Robbins of Porcupine Press for their professionalism and support in the publication process. Further, thanks are due to friends, acquaintances, some of my former colleagues, and some family members who travelled along with or alongside my journey, and I with theirs, for some shorter or longer periods of time in my life.

Then there's the software. Many programmers tirelessly write open source software for all to inspect and use. I'd like to thank the developers of Miktex and TeXnicCenter, since most of this book was written in LaTeX. A, final, two-edged-sword sort of thanks is due to the South African government who enforced stringent COVID-19 curfews that made me have to sit at home more often than I would have liked.

www.ingramcontent.com/pod-product-compliance
Lightning Source LLC
Chambersburg PA
CBHW031219050326
40689CB00009B/1399